Folk Elements in Burmese Buddhism

Folk Elements
in Burmese Buddhism

MAUNG HTIN AUNG

London
OXFORD UNIVERSITY PRESS
Bombay . New York . Karachi
1962

Oxford University Press, Amen House, London E.C. 4

GLASGOW NEW YORK TORONTO MELBOURNE WELLINGTON
BOMBAY CALCUTTA MADRAS KARACHI LAHORE DACCA
CAPE TOWN SALISBURY NAIROBI IBADAN ACCRA
KUALA LUMPUR HONG KONG

Printed in Great Britain

PREFACE

Chapters 2 to 8 were originally given as lectures to the Burma Research Society, Rangoon, at its annual meetings from 1952 to 1957. They have, of course, been rewritten, but traces of the spoken word remain here and there, and occasionally the same facts given in an earlier chapter are repeated in a later chapter, for which defects I crave the reader's indulgence.

I had promised my publishers, the Oxford University Press, to submit the manuscript of this book by June 1958, but other preoccupations intervened and some years passed before I could do so. I am grateful to them for their patience. In the meantime, I wrote an essay on the subject for *Perspective of Burma* in 1958. I am grateful to Intercultural Publications Inc., New York, for permission to reproduce that essay as Chapter 1 of this book.

MAUNG HTIN AUNG

FOREWORD

One full moon day, some thirty-five years ago, I was attending the annual festival of a 'Jungle' pagoda some miles outside the town of Pegu. The pagoda was reputed to be the place where the two monks, Dhamma-zedi and Dhammapala, practised magic, and the place was full of persons, mostly impostors, who claimed to be following the path of purity and endeavour, along which Dhamma-zedi had travelled before them. I watched with some amusement a white-clad and bearded figure walking by, surrounded by a crowd of devotees, but I stopped smiling when I saw an incongruous figure among them, namely a young student, wearing a brand-new college blazer. My surprise turned into shock when I recognized him to be young Maung Htin Aung who had just entered University College, Rangoon, with a very brilliant academic record behind him. I was by then a lecturer in chemistry, and shouted to him rather angrily, 'What do you think you are doing here?' and he replied, 'I am doing research, sir, in unnatural science.' 'I hope you will publish a thesis on it,' I said with due sarcasm, and he replied, 'I will, sir, if you will please write the introduction.' Years passed, he became my colleague on the University staff, and in 1946 he became the Rector. He had by then published his *Burmese Drama* and his *Burmese Folk-Tales* and I reminded him of our encounter at the Jungle pagoda and suggested that he should now write his thesis on unnatural science. 'Sir, please do not remind me of a mis-spent youth,' he replied. But a few weeks later, he came to me with a handful of Burmese alchemic compounds and discussed their composition.

The account of the pre-Buddhist religious cults which are

contained in the following pages was originally given as lectures by Dr. Htin Aung to the annual meetings of the Burma Research Society during the period 1952 to 1958, in his capacity, first as Vice-President, then as President, and finally as Past President of the Society. I had the honour and the privilege of listening to all the lectures, and I can still remember the excitement and the controversy that followed his first lecture in the series, which was on Burmese Initiation Ceremonies. Some members of the audience were shocked at his defence of the Ari monks, and the one-hour lecture was followed by a heated discussion which lasted for some three hours. The following year, his lecture on the Nine Gods resulted not only in controversy, but also in resentment against him for endeavouring to show that the ceremony was not really Buddhistic in origin. However, as further lectures followed, his audiences came to appreciate his findings.

I have no hesitation in saying that Dr. Htin Aung has rendered again a signal service to Burmese studies in publishing his lectures in book form. Apart from his academic attainments, Dr. Htin Aung is specially qualified to write on the subject of the pre-Buddhist religion of the Burmese, because he combines in his person a deep understanding and faith in Theravada Buddhism and a sympathy and appreciation of the aspirations of the Burmese astrologer and the Burmese alchemist. Belonging to a family one of whose ancestors is listed among the Thirty-seven *Nats*, he was kidnapped as a child by a village headman and initiated into the cult of the were-tiger; this background will perhaps explain his sympathetic attitude towards the folk elements in Burmese Buddhism. Just as his *Burmese Drama* and his *Burmese Folk-Tales* placed on permanent record many Burmese oral traditions that have now completely disappeared even

from the remotest village, this book puts on permanent record
the oral lore of the pre-Buddhist cults, which has never been
collected before, even in the Burmese language.

U Po Tha
Professor of Chemistry, and
Dean of the Faculty of Engineering

University of Rangoon,
1st October, 1959.

CONTENTS

1

Folk Elements in Burmese Buddhism

WHEN the great king Anawrahta of Pagan united the whole of Burma into a single kingdom in the eleventh century and made Theravada Buddhism the national religion, there were already in existence a number of primitive religious cults, the most important and the most popular of which were the worship of *Nat* spirits, astrology, and alchemy. In addition, although the Theravada Buddhism which had flourished in the earlier kingdom of Prome had died out long before, there also existed Mahayana Buddhism and Tantric (or magical) Buddhism; according to the Chronicles, however, these were debased and distorted, bearing strange fruit from the fertile soil of native cults of magic and sorcery. All the different cults were given an artificial unity by the fact that they were all under the patronage of the Ari monks. These Ari monks had some acquaintance with the Buddhist scriptures, gloried in the name of the Buddha, and wore dark-brown robes and conical hats. But they also presided over the *Nat* spirit festivals, at which hundreds of animals were sacrificed.[1]

Astrology to the Burmese meant not only the methods of tracing the courses of the planets and their influence on mortals, but also the ritual by which the planets were appeased and made to withdraw their baneful influence. In other words, it involved a worship of the planets. As Burmese astrology had its origins in Hindu astrology, so the worship of the planets involved worship of at least some of the Hindu gods.

[1] For further details of the Ari monks see Chapter 9.

1

Alchemy also came to Burma from India but Burmese alchemy became a religious cult. The Burmese alchemist did not merely seek the power to transmute base metals into gold, he also had the noble aim of evolving an eternally youthful body, which would be an answer to the perpetual human lament that beauty and youth must pass.

The worship of *Nats* was purely native in origin and developed out of that form of animism which still prevails among some of the hill peoples of the country. The term *Nat* originally meant a lord and involved an idea similar to feudal overlordship. A *Nat* was a spirit who had some dominion over a group of people or over a certain object or objects. The spirit who had dominion over a small withered tree was as much a *Nat* as the spirit who had dominion over a particular village or district. The suzerainty of a *Nat* was both territorial and personal. The *Nat* guardian of a village had power over all those who were born in the village or born of a village family, wherever they might be, and he also had power over all who came to his village during the time they remained there. He would inflict no harm, nay, he would even give his protection to those who recognized his suzerainty, and such recognition could be expressed by an offering of rice or fruit, a few words of supplication or a gesture of homage.

At first the *Nats* who were worshipped were impersonal and local, as, for example, the *Nats* of the banyan tree, the hill, and the lake which were just outside the village, and the guardian *Nat* of the village. Later on, thirty-six personal and national *Nats* came into being who were distinct personages with their own life histories and who were worshipped all over the country. They did not replace the local *Nats*, but diminished their importance.

The most important of the thirty-six were the Lord of the Great Mountain and his sister Lady Golden-Face, whose abode was on Mount Popa, an extinct volcano in central Burma. They became, in the ninth century, the guardian gods of the city of Pagan and its kings. There was an annual *Nat* feast on Mount Popa itself, at which hundreds of animals were offered as sacrifice to the Lord of the Great Mountain and Lady Golden-Face. People came from afar to take part in the feast, to get drunk with ecstasy and toddy-wine, and to dance with abandon, believing themselves to have become possessed by the *Nats*. There were spirit mediums in attendance at the *Nat* shrines who provided the wild music and led the wilder dances. The Popa feast was held on a full moon day in December, just as on other full moon days there were also feasts connected with other pre-Buddhist cults.

When Anawrahta made Theravada Buddhism the national religion of the country there was opposition from the Aris, as could be expected, and because they exercised great influence over the people, the king had no choice but to resort to religious persecution. The Ari monks were unfrocked and made to serve in the royal armies. All the images of the gods of the planets and the Hindu gods were seized and placed in a Vishnu temple, which was renamed 'the Prison of the Gods'. All the pre-Buddhist cults were suppressed. Spirit mediums left the shrines to become strolling musicians, dancers, and actors.

But the people found it difficult to discard old beliefs and old practices immediately and resorted to stratagem. The followers of the cult of alchemy modified their conception of an eternally youthful body to that of a body remaining youthful for thousands of years in order to conform to the Buddhist doctrine that nothing is permanent, and justified their search for the elixir of youth by saying that they wanted to live until the coming of the next Buddha so that they could listen to his preaching. The followers of the cult of astrology threw a veneer of Buddhism over their ritual and ceremony, as, for example, in the case of the ceremony of the Nine Gods, where the gods of the nine planets gave way to Buddha and his eight disciples.

As for *Nat* worship, the people, in spite of the king's edicts, went on worshipping the *Nats*, and Anawrahta finally decided to bring them over into Buddhism. The figures of the Thirty-six Lords were taken from their shrines and placed in the king's great pagoda in an attitude of worship; he declared that the number was now thirty-seven, because Sakra, the king of the gods and guardian of Buddhism, was at the head of the pantheon. The cult of Thirty-six Lords, therefore, became the cult of the Thirty-seven Lords, and Anawrahta replaced some of the earlier lords with the *Nat* spirits of some of his dead heroes.

All this was possible mainly because the Burmese concept of the *Nat* was a very comprehensive one and took in under its wing Hindu gods as well as Buddhist figures. As the *Nats* themselves were now shown to be worshippers of the Buddha it was deemed proper for Buddhists to worship the *Nats*. The feasts of the full moon became festivals of the full moon on being given a coating of Buddhism, just as pre-Christian feasts of spring and midwinter in Europe became the great Christian festivals of Easter and Christmas.

With the passing of time people came to forget the pre-Buddhist and primitive origins of their folk beliefs in alchemy, astrology, and *Nats*, and learned to accept them as part of their Buddhism, just as they thought that the pre-Buddhist belief in the transmigration of souls was a doctrine of Theravada Buddhism. Thus at the present time many Burmese (in rural and primitive areas the majority) still consult their astrologer and make their offerings to the *Nats*, without ceasing to be good Buddhists. At certain times of the year, dances are still held through which the dancers try to become possessed by the *Nat* spirits; a few Burmese still even make alchemic experiments.

But such beliefs and practices cannot overwhelm Buddhism in any way for they have been shorn of their primitive meaning and philosophy. The Burmese who resort to astrology,

4

alchemy, or *Nat* worship do so for safety and success in their mundane life, and the same Burmese will observe the Buddhist religious days and perform deeds of merit in preparation for the countless existences that they must undergo in the whirlpool of rebirth.

In the following pages an attempt is made to consider, first, the folk elements that exist in Burmese Buddhism at the present day, and then to trace their origins in the native cults which were flourishing in A.D. 1056 when the heavy hand of Anawrahta fell on them.

2

The Nine Gods

Preparations for the ceremony

The ceremony of the Nine Gods is usually held when there is sickness in the house. As in the case of all Burmese ceremonies it begins with the issue of invitations by the head of the household to relations and friends. In the villages, of course, the invitation is to the whole village. A master of ceremonies is then engaged for a fee. In villages he is an amateur, but in towns he is a professional and is known as the '*Saya* of the Nine-Gods Ceremony'. The Burmese term *Saya* means a 'Master Craftsman' and usually the craft that he practises is attached to his term of *Saya*, as, for example, '*Saya* of the School' (a teacher), '*Saya* of the University', '*Saya* of Medicine', '*Saya* of Magic', '*Saya* of Astrology', '*Saya* of Carpentry', '*Saya* of Masonry', '*Saya* of Pot-Making', '*Saya* of Machines', etc. That there should be a *Saya* to perform the ceremony of the Nine Gods is surprising since Burmese Buddhist ceremonies do not need a priest to act as the medium between the worshipper and the worshipped, and Burmese *phongyis* are monks and not priests in fact.

Invitations are issued in the morning and the 'Master' is engaged from the morning, although the ceremony will begin only in the evening. The Master spends the whole day in making a miniature monastery of banana stem, and in making paper umbrellas, paper flag-poles with streamers, and paper prayer-flags. In towns, however, the Master has a ready-made miniature monastery of wood. In the evening, when darkness has fallen, the Master of the Ceremony comes to the house

7

with all his paraphernalia and, in the front room, he sets up his monastery.

The eight Arahats

The monastery is placed at the eastern end of the front room, and it is imperative that it faces due west. The cardinal points are of the utmost importance in the ceremony. The audience will be facing the monastery and, therefore, facing east. The Master then sets up the images that he has brought with him. Right in the centre of the monastery he places the image of the Buddha, and he places the images of eight of his Chief Disciples (all *Arahats*) at the cardinal points of the monastery and with the faces turned towards the Buddha:

North-east	*East*	*South-east*
Rahula	Kodanna	Revata
North	*Centre*	*South*
Moggallana	Buddha	Sariputta
North-west	*West*	*South-west*
Gavampati	Ananda	Upali

Of the eight *Arahats*, six are well known to all Buddhists, but two, Revata and Gavampati, are not so frequently mentioned in the Buddhist scriptures. Sariputta and Moggallana were the Chief and Vice-Chief Disciples of the Buddha. They were friends, born to luxury and riches, and together they renounced the world and sought for the true faith, until they met the Buddha. By that time the Buddha had established his Order and there were already many members, but because of their special purity and saintliness they were appointed First and Second Chief Disciples.

Sariputta was in his wisdom next only to the Buddha himself. Moggallana was famous for his supernatural powers, and using these powers he often visited the abode of the Gods and the various other worlds of the universe; he even subjugated the Great *Naga* of Mount Mayyu and once scolded Sakra, King of the Gods, and the Great God, Bramah Baka.

Kodanna was one of the eight Brahmin astrologers who were invited by the king, the Buddha's father, to prognosticate the future of his new-born son, and while the other seven foretold that the child would become either the Buddha or the emperor of the universe, Kodanna alone announced that the child would become the Buddha definitely. Confident in his own prophecy he renounced the world and, becoming a recluse in the forest, he awaited the appearance of the Buddha. He was one of the 'Five Recluses' to whom the Buddha preached the First Sermon, and who became, therefore, the first members of the Buddha's Order. He later retired to the forest and lived alone for twelve years, waited upon by thousands of wild elephants.

Ananda was a cousin and the attendant of the Buddha. He was so busy attending on the Buddha that he had no time to meditate and become an *Arahat* during the Buddha's lifetime. He was well-loved by monks and laymen alike because of his humility and good-nature. When the Buddha lay dying, surrounded by *Arahats* and Gods, Ananda was human enough to cry like a child until the Buddha consoled him. Upali was the barber to the prince cousins of the Buddha, and when his masters renounced the world he also followed suit. He became the chief authority on the *Vinaya*, or the rules of discipline of the Order. Rahula was the Buddha's only son and was received into the Order when he was still a child; after becoming an *Arahat* he became one of the Chief Disciples on his own purity and merit.

Revata and Gavampati were also possessors of unusual supernatural powers. Revata once created, by his supernatural powers, splendid monasteries for the Buddha and his monks while they were passing through a wilderness, and Gavampati once stopped the tide and thus saved some monks from drowning as they slept on a sand-bank. Revata was the youngest brother of Sariputta, and although he made his abode in the forest he used to come and visit the Buddha and Sariputta regularly. He was later declared by the Buddha to be the foremost of the forest-dwelling monks of his Order. As he foresaw that his end was approaching he went and visited the Buddha and Sariputta for the last time, and on his way back to the forest he was mistaken for a thief by some king's officials and arrested and taken to their master. Revata now announced that he was a monk and an *Arahat*, and sitting cross-legged in the air he preached a sermon to the king. As he finished his sermon he died and flames rose out of his body and consumed it.

Gavampati was a god with a golden palace before he was born as Gavampati, but unlike other palaces which disappeared with the death of their gods, this palace did not disappear; Gavampati, in fact, used to spend much of his time in his old age in this palace among the gods, and he was there when he was invited to come and participate in the First Synod, held soon after the Buddha's death. He realized, however, that his own death was imminent and after making an offering to the Order of his begging-bowl and his robes, he died. According to purely Mon and Burmese tradition (i.e. not according to the general Buddhist tradition), Gavampati in a previous birth was a native of Lower Burma; he was hatched from an egg laid by a *Naga*-Princess after her union with an alchemist, but he died when he was only ten years of age; when he was later reborn as Gavampati and became an *Arahat* he remembered his previous life, and on his invitation the Buddha himself visited the kingdom of Thaton in Lower Burma. According to another local tradition Gavampati did not die at the time of the First Synod, and he even assisted in the foundation of the Pyu city of Prome. The special supernatural powers attributed to Revata and Gavampati impressed the early Burmese. Revata was adopted as their patron saint by the magicians, alchemists, hermits, and monks who dwelt in the Burmese forest performing austerities, and Gavampati became the patron saint of the Mons and the Pyus.

The gods of the planets

After placing the images of the above-mentioned *Arahats* in position, the Master of the Ceremony now sets up the figures of the gods of the planets. Burmese astrology recognizes the seven planets, namely, Sun, Moon, Mars, Jupiter, Mercury, Venus, and Saturn. In addition, it recognizes two other planets, Rahu and Kate. All the Burmese names of the planets are borrowed from Hindu astrology, but the Burmese Rahu and Kate are different from the Hindu Rahu and Kate. The Burmese consider them to be distinct and separate planets, whereas Hindu astrology considers them to be either the Dragon's Head and Tail, or the Ascending and Descending Nodes. To the Burmese, Kate is the king of all the planets.

As with other nations the Burmese name the seven days of their week after the seven planets, but Burmese astrology recognizes an eight-day week, Wednesday being divided into two days; until 6 p.m. it is Wednesday, but from 6 p.m. to midnight it is Rahu's day.

Just as the gods of Hindu mythology ride on particular animals as their 'vehicles', the nine Burmese planets have their own animal vehicles and are often represented by these animals:

1. Sunday planet rides on a *Galon*, the Burmese name for the Pali *Garuda*, a mythical bird, who is the eternal enemy of the *Naga*.

11

2. Monday planet rides on a tiger.
3. Tuesday planet rides on a lion.
4. Wednesday planet rides on an elephant with tusks.
5. Rahu's planet rides on a tuskless elephant (tuskless elephants are believed to be more powerful than elephants with tusks).
6. Thursday planet rides on a rat.
7. Friday planet rides on a guinea pig.[1]
8. Saturday planet rides on a *Naga*.
9. Kate planet rides on an 'Animal of Five Beauties', a mythical animal with the antlers of a deer, the tusks and trunk of an elephant, the mane of a lion, the body of a *Naga*, and the tail of a fish.

The figures now being set are those of the gods of the planets astride their animals. The Master places the figures of

North-east Sunday Sun	*East* Monday Moon	*South-east* Tuesday Mars
North Friday Venus	Kate	*South* Wednesday (day) Mercury
North-west Wednesday (night) Rahu	*West* Thursday Jupiter	*South-west* Saturday Saturn

[1] According to astrological beliefs prevailing among the Shans, the Friday planet rides on an ox.

the Kate planet in the centre of the monastery but behind
the Buddha. The other eight planets have their cardinal
points and each is placed behind an *Arahat* as shown in the
table on p. 12. From their cardinal points, and behind
the *Arahats*, the figures of the planets face towards the
Buddha.

The Five Great Gods

Then the Master sets up his last group of figures. They are
five in number representing the Five Great Gods, namely:
Thurathati, Sandi, Paramay-thwa, Maha-Peinne, Peikthano
or Gawra-manta.

All these goddesses and gods are Hindu in origin. Thurathati is the Hindu goddess Saraswati, the consort of Brahma;
Sandi is Chandi, the consort of Siva; Paramay-thwa is Siva
himself; Maha-Peinne is the Burmese name for Ganesh,[1] the
elephant-headed god; Peikthano is Vishnu, and Gawra-
manta or 'he with the horse' is the ninth (and future) incar-
nation of Vishnu. As in the case of the eight *Arahats*, and the
nine gods of the planets, the figures of the Hindu gods are
carved in an attitude of worship, and they are set in line
facing the Buddha in front of the little monastery. Thurathati is on the extreme left of the line and Siva is therefore in
the centre. It is to be noticed that Thurathati's consort,
Brahma, is absent, and Vishnu's consort, the gentle Lakshmi,
is also absent.

The ceremony begins

On the roof of the miniature monastery there fly nine miniature prayer-flags and streamers from the nine miniature
poles, and there are also nine miniature golden umbrellas.
The largest prayer-flag, pole (with streamers) and golden

[1] The Burmese Ganesh and the other Hindu gods are considered in detail
in Chapter 3.

umbrella are above the Buddha, and the remaining eight flags, poles and umbrellas are above the *Arahats* and the gods at the eight cardinal points, and are of the same size. The five Hindu gods do not have these insignias of worship.

The Master of the Ceremony now places nine miniature flower-pots in position, the flower-pot placed before the Buddha being the largest, the other eight of equal size. He then places in position nine miniature begging-bowls, the largest in front of the Buddha, the remaining eight of equal size before the eight *Arahats*, and nine miniature plates, the largest in front of the Kate planet and the other eight of equal size before the gods of the other planets. The flower-pots contain three kinds of flowers each but the begging-bowls and the plates are empty. Finally he sets up nine beeswax candles at the nine points and lights them. He then starts to recite extracts from Buddhist texts and offers special prayers on behalf of the household.

By this time the guests have arrived. They kneel before the monastery and make obeisance. The guests are served with light refreshments: in villages pickled tea and plain tea, in towns ice-cream and cakes. It is a social occasion and the guests chat and laugh. At about nine or ten o'clock the guests leave, the inmates retire to their bedrooms, and the Master of the Ceremony is left alone in the room, still chanting extracts from the scriptures. At midnight he, too, goes to sleep in a makeshift bed in the room.

About an hour before dawn the inmates get up and prepare the food to be offered to the Nine Gods. Three kinds of fruit, usually banana, coco-nut, and plum, and three kinds of jam are kept ready. The rice to be offered to the Buddha and the *Arahats* is cooked in an earthen pot which has never been used before, and the rice to be offered to the gods of the planets is cooked separately in another new earthen pot. At dawn, the begging-bowls before the Buddha and the *Arahats* and the plates before the gods are filled with three kinds of fruit,

14

three kinds of jam, and cooked rice. The Master of the Ceremony first chants some more extracts from Buddhist texts
and offers the alms-food to the Buddha and the *Arahats*. Then
he invokes the gods of the planets to come and accept it.
He recites a particular formula of invocation for each planet,
in the following order: Sunday, Monday, Tuesday, Wednesday, Saturday, Thursday, Rahu, Friday, Kate.

It will be noticed that the gods of the planets are invoked
in the order of the cardinal points, and that the chief planet,
Kate, is invoked last. After the gods of the planets have been
invoked, the Master of the Ceremony remains silent for a few
minutes and then he recites the formula of dispersal. Again
for each planet a particular formula is used, but the order is
changed, as follows: Sunday, Tuesday, Saturday, Rahu,
Monday, Wednesday, Thursday, Friday, Kate.

The Sunday, Tuesday, Saturday, and Rahu planets are
considered by the Burmese to be Malefics, or planets with an
evil influence, and the Monday, Wednesday, Thursday and
Friday planets are considered to be Benefics, or planets with
a benign influence. Kate is considered to be the most powerful
and a Benefic, but as the chief planet it cannot be grouped
with the other planets.[1] Thus the four Malefics are dispersed
first, then the four Benefics, and finally the Kate planet.
Another explanation is the astrological belief that at the
beginning of this universe the nine planets appeared one by
one in this order. The formula of dispersal is really a formula
of expulsion or exorcism. And with it the ceremony closes.

Explanations of the ceremony

With all Burmese ceremonies there is a Buddhist explanation, and a story from the *Dhammapada Commentary* is cited
as the basis of the ceremony of the Nine Gods.

A Brahman, his wife, and their little son saluted a monk,

---

[1] Although Kate remains important in the ritual of the Nine Gods,
modern Burmese astrology tends to ignore it.

who said 'Live long!' to both parents, but remained silent to the little son.

Said the father, 'Reverend Sir, why was it that when we saluted you, you said, "Live long!" But when this boy saluted you, you said not a word?' 'Some disaster awaits this boy, Brahman.' 'How long will he live, Reverend Sir?' 'For seven days, Brahman.' 'Is there any way of averting this, Reverend Sir?' 'I know of no way of averting this.' 'But who might know, Reverend Sir?' 'The monk Gotama; go to him and ask him.' 'Were I to go there, I should be afraid because of having abandoned my austerities.' 'If you love your son, think not of having abandoned your austerities, but go to him and ask him.'

The Brahman went to the Teacher, and himself straightway saluted him. 'Live long!' said the Teacher. When the boy's mother saluted him, he said the same. But when they made the boy salute him, he held his peace. Then the Brahman asked the Teacher the same question he had previously asked the monk, and the Teacher made the same prediction. The Brahman asked the Teacher, 'Reverend Sir, is there no way of averting this?' 'There might be, Brahman.' 'What way might there be, Reverend Sir?'

'If you erect a pavilion before the door of your house, and set a chair in the centre of it, and arrange eight or sixteen seats in a circle about it, and cause my disciples to sit therein; and if you then cause texts to be recited for the purpose of securing protection and averting evil consequences for the space of seven days uninterruptedly, in that case the danger that threatens him might be averted.' 'Sir Gotama, it is a perfectly easy matter to erect a pavilion and do all the rest, but how am I to obtain the services of your disciples?' 'If you will do all this, I will send my disciples.' 'Very well, Sir Gotama.'

So the Brahman completed all of the preparations at the door of his house and then went to the Teacher. The Teacher sent the monks, and they went and sat down, seating the boy also on a little bench. For seven nights and seven days without interruption, the monks recited the usual texts, and on the seventh day the Teacher came himself. When the Teacher came, the deities of all the worlds assembled. But a certain ogre named Avaruddhaka,

16

who had served Vessavana for twelve years and who had received
the boon, 'Seven days hence you shall receive this boy', approached
and stood awaiting. But when the Teacher came there, and the
powerful deities gathered themselves together, and the weak
deities drew back stepping back twelve leagues so as to make
room, then Avaruddhaka stepped back also.

The Teacher recited the Protective Texts all night long, with
the result that when the seven days had elapsed, Avaruddhaka
failed to get the boy. Indeed, when the dawn of the eighth day
rose, they brought the boy and caused him to make obeisance to
the Teacher. Said the Teacher, 'Live long!' 'Sir Gotama, how long
will the boy live?' 'For a hundred and twenty years, Brahman.'
So they gave him the name of Lad-Whose-Years-Increased,
Ayuvaddhana.[1]

That the explanation is an afterthought seems obvious.
The *Dhammapada* story does mention eight or sixteen monks
seated round the Buddha, but they did not sit in the form of a
square but a circle. The story makes no mention of the planets.
Moreover, the story of the Nine Gods contains elements which
can have no Buddhistic explanation.

The full name of the ceremony means 'Offering of Alms-
food to the Nine Buddhas.' It will be noticed, however, that
there are only one Buddha and eight *Arahats*. *Phaya*, the
Burmese word for Buddha, can never be applied to a monk,
even if he be an *Arahat*, but before the introduction of
Buddhism it could mean a god, and so the real meaning of the
Burmese word *Phaya-kozu* would seem to be the Nine Gods.
If that is so, the Nine Gods must mean the nine planets, and
in the ceremony the gods of the nine planets are, in fact,
being worshipped, although that fact is hidden underneath a
coating of Buddhism.

In the ceremony no special prayers or scriptures are prescribed for the worship and offering of alms-food to the Buddha
and the eight *Arahats*. The Master of the Ceremony chooses

---

[1] Burlingame, *Buddhist Legends*, Part II (Harvard Oriental Series).

the prayers and the scriptures at his discretion, but certain set formulas of worship and offering for the nine planets are prescribed, and the Master of the Ceremony must recite those particular formulas. The Buddha and the *Arahats* are never invoked nor dispersed, but the nine gods are not only invoked but carefully dispersed.

That the ceremony has some Hindu origin is illustrated by the presence of the figures of the five Hindu gods and goddesses, although no prayers nor offerings are made to them, and by the fact that the alms-food offered does not include any meat. To the more devout Masters of the Ceremony the combination of the worship of the Buddha and the *Arahats*, on the one hand, and that of the planets, on the other, seems so incongruous that occasionally one finds such a Master using a miniature monastery for the Buddha and the *Arahats* and a miniature one-roomed house for the planets; he calls the monastery 'the Buddha's Monastery' and the house 'the Planet's House'.

Hindu astrology was known and practised in Burma before A.D. 1056, and the Chronicles tell of two reforms of the Burmese calendar in A.D. 78 and A.D. 640 respectively, according to astrological predictions and requirements. Even at the present day Hindu astrology, necessarily modified by Burmese beliefs, still holds sway in the mind of the average Burmese, who often consults a professional astrologer.

The basic belief of Burmese astrology is that the planets, except Kate, mould a man's fate. The planet of a man's birthday will be the main guardian of his fate, but at each particular period of a man's life a particular planet throws upon him its baneful or its beneficial influence. For example, at one period of his life he will be under the influence of Saturn and ill-fortune will befall him, but at another period he will be under the influence of Venus and good fortune will result. Thus the ebb and flow of a man's fortune depends on the paths in the sky of the planets. The Burmese chronicles

18

always mention the particular day of the week on which each king was born, and until the last two decades the name of a Burmese indicated upon which day of the week he was born.

The letters of the Burmese alphabet were divided up between the eight planets thus:

ka, kha, ga, gha, nga	—Monday
sa, hsa, za, zha, nya	—Tuesday
ta, hta, da, dha, na	—Saturday
pa, hpa, ba, bha, ma	—Thursday
la, wa	—Wednesday
ya, ra	—Rahu's day
tha, ha	—Friday

and on this division a person's name was chosen. Thus, the first name of a Saturday-born would begin with one of the following letters: ta, hta, da, dha, na

as, for example, 'Tin', 'Htin', 'Nan'. This custom of naming a person after his birthday planet has now fallen into disuse, except in old-fashioned families.

The Burmese pagoda, like the ceremony of the Nine Gods, retains under a Buddhistic colouring the cult of the planet gods. The eight cardinal points round a pagoda are named after the planets, and the terms east, west, north, south, south-east, south-west, north-east and north-west are never used to refer to the various points of the pagoda; instead the following terms are used:

the Sunday corner (north-east)
the Monday corner (east)
the Tuesday corner (south-east)
the Wednesday corner (south)
the Saturday corner (south-west)
the Thursday corner (west)
the Rahu corner (north-west)
the Friday corner (north)

A person who has been told by the astrologer that he is under the baneful influence of a Malefic offers special prayers at the 'corner' of that particular planet. He will also offer special prayers at the corner of his own birthday planet. It will be noticed that the Kate planet is absent. The original reason for this can only be guessed. Perhaps it was found difficult to put the Kate planet right in the centre, or perhaps, as the fortunes of a man never fell directly under this planet's influence, no special prayers to the Kate planet were considered necessary. Each of the eight corners of the pagoda has a sign, which depicts not the particular god astride his animal, but the animal itself.

All the above facts will indicate that there existed a magico-religious cult connected with the worship of the planets before Buddhism became the official religion of the Burmese. A Chinese chronicle of the ninth century, the *Man-Shu*, mentioned the presence in Burma of 'many fortune tellers and astrologers'. The cult was, of course, Hindu in origin, but whether it was superimposed on an existing native cult is a matter for consideration.

Leaving aside the mythical and composite animal that the Kate planet rides, the animals ridden by the other eight gods are real animals to the Burmese mind. Although the *Naga* and the *Galon* are mythical animals, the average Burmese villager still believes that they are real animals living in the depths of the forests of Burma. The conception of these animal-vehicles of the planets is Hindu in origin but Burmese in development. It has been noted that the signs at the eight corners of a pagoda depict not the planet-gods but the animals. It may therefore be that the cult of the nine planets took over for its support an existing native animal cult. Just as the *Naga*[1] was worshipped, perhaps the other seven animals also were once worshipped by the Burmese. It may be also that there was a native cult connected with the mystic number nine. Of

[1] The worship of the *Naga* is considered in the appendix to Chapter 7.

course with most peoples of the world nine is a mystic number, and to the Buddhist it is also a mystic number because the Buddha has 'nine special attributes'. However, there is some evidence that with the Burmese there was a definite magico-religious cult connected with the number. The Burmese word *ko* can mean both 'nine' and 'to seek protection by worshipping', and the Burmese phrase *Nat-ko* means to 'offer (food) to the *Nat* to get his protection'. In making offerings to a *Nat*, nine candles, nine dishes of food or nine kinds of food are often used. With the Ceremony of the Nine Gods, although the nine candles, the nine-flower pots, etc., can be explained away as being merely consequential to the fact that the gods were nine in number, it is to be noted that nine kinds of offering are made, leaving aside the rice, namely: three kinds of flowers, three kinds of fruit, and three kinds of jam.

The popular Burmese card game *Ko-Mee* or 'Nine Fires', success at which depends entirely on chance and not on skill, was originally a ritual game connected with the mystic number nine. In addition, there were 'nine districts' of Kyaukse in Upper Burma, and in these districts, even at the present day, the number nine must be avoided, as the *Nats* will be angry if their special number is used by human beings. For example, if a caravan of nine carts goes on a trading venture, a dire accident will result, if one builds a house on the ninth waxing or waning of a Burmese month, disaster will follow, and if one goes out with eight companions, sorrow will result.

But whether the cult of the Nine Planets was superimposed on existing native cults or otherwise it was definitely non-Buddhist, and all non-Buddhist religious cults, whether native or alien in origin, were suppressed after Buddhism became the official religion of the Burmese under Anawrahta. For a non-Buddhist cult to survive it was necessary to give it a colouring of Buddhism, and also to admit that the gods of the cult were inferior to the Buddha and were supporters of the new religion. The cult of the Nine Planets had to bow to the new order of things. The Ceremony of the Nine Planets was transformed into the joint-ceremony of the worship of the Buddha and the eight *Arahats,* and the worship of the Nine Planets. Admission that its gods were inferior to the Buddha and were supporters of the new religion was made by carving the figures of the Nine Planets and the Five Hindu Gods and Goddesses in an attitude of worship, and by placing them with their faces turned towards the image of the Buddha. At first, of course, there could have been no real change of heart, and in secret many devotees at the new ceremony would be worshipping the old gods of the planets. But as centuries passed and Buddhism gradually became firmly rooted in the life of the Burmese people, the anti-Buddhist and the pre-Buddhist elements in the ceremony gradually receded to the background.

3

The Feast of the New Year

The visit of Thagyamin

Since the beginning of March the weather has been hot and dry and the whole countryside lies parched and barren. The harvest has been gathered and celebrated at the festival of the full moon of Tabaung in March (this Tabaung festival is a Buddhist festival now, but in the remote past it used to be a harvest festival). It is now nearly the middle of April, and the Burmese cultivator, like his paddy field and his plough-oxen, finds the weather trying and the enforced holiday monotonous. But there is excitement in the air, for the Feast of the New Year is swiftly approaching. The astrologers have published broadsheets in which the details of the New Year are given. The King of the Gods, Thagyamin, is coming down to the earth on his annual visit. He will come and spend the last two days (sometimes three) of the old year in the abode of the human beings, and the exact moment of his departure will bring in the New Year. The Feast lasts for three days (sometimes four), and the day of his arrival is known as the Day of Descent, the day of his departure the Day of Ascent, and the day in between (sometimes two days in between) the Day of Sojourn. During these three days (or four days) elderly people fast and keep the Eight Precepts or Ten Precepts and go to the monasteries and pagodas to offer alms-food.

At home, the housewife prepares cooling drinks and sweet cakes to be sent as presents to the neighbours. The children are warned to be on their best behaviour, for the King of the Gods, Thagyamin, brings with him two big volumes, one bound in dog-skin, the other in gold, and he records in the dog-skin book the names of those who have committed misdeeds during the course of the year, and in the gold book the names of those who have performed acts of merit. The exact times of the arrival and departure of the god, which have been calculated and proclaimed in the broadsheets, will be signalled by the booming of cannons and firing of guns under the supervision of the relevant administrative official of government, and on the front porch of every house there stand the New Year pots filled with special flowers and special leaves to welcome the visiting god. At the exact time of his arrival the head of the household lifts up the pots towards the sky as a gesture of homage, and at the exact time of his departure the head of the household pours out slowly the water from the pots on to the ground with a prayer for good fortune, good rainfall and good harvest for the coming year. As both the husband and the wife are joint heads of the family these ceremonies are performed either by the husband or the wife or by both, and are performed simply and quietly.

But outside the house there is very little quiet, for the Feast of the New Year is also the merry Festival of Water. Since dawn, teams of young men and young women have been occupying strategic points on the roadsides with pails and buckets of water. Groups of young men and young women are also to be found in the gaily decorated temporary structures which have sprung up almost overnight at every street corner, in which, in addition to pots and cans of water, there are all kinds of sweet cakes and cool drinks for all the passers-by and the merry-makers. No passer-by will escape the drenching, no matter whether he or she is a Buddhist or non-Buddhist, Burmese or non-Burmese. Only the monks and the sick and the infirm are spared the deluge. Gaily dressed young men and young women in decorated cars or carts drive round the town or village, throwing water and getting drenched in return. Sometimes a band of young men will challenge another group of young men or a group of young women to throw more water on them by shouting slogans and singing songs. In this merry-making the equality between sexes[1] is forgotten and the advantage is given to the young women, who, therefore, tend to become more boisterous than the men. A team of young women is permitted to 'capture' a young man who throws water upon them, and when he is caught his face is blackened with oil and soot and his hands are tied together, and he is given ducking after ducking until he admits defeat by performing the 'monkey dance'.

After three days of boisterous water-throwing and hectic merry-making, peace and decorum prevail on the day following the Day of Ascent, which is commonly called New Year's Day, although technically the New Year has begun at the actual moment of the god's departure. People now wash their hair with a sweet-smelling shampoo specially prepared from a tree bark, bathe themselves in scented water, and, putting on their finest silken clothes, they go to the pagodas and monasteries to worship. Many buy live fishes, meant for killing by the fishmongers, and set them free in nearby lakes and rivers, with prayers for long life. Gifts of flowers, fruits and candles are taken in person to one's parents, elders, and teachers. This New Year's Day and the actual period of the Water Festival, notwithstanding its riotous merry-making, are considered very auspicious, and people endeavour specially not to break the Five Precepts, and also to refrain from cutting down trees and plants, assaulting people and beating animals, weeping and wailing, blood-letting, eating oil and spices, transacting in goods and money, and sending out heralds, envoys, agents, and messengers.

The ceremonial hair-washing

Until a few decades ago the ceremonial washing of hair was as important as the throwing of water. For purposes of

[1] In Burmese society, women have equal legal and social rights with men.

25

the ceremonial hair-washing people were divided into three classes, those who were born on the same day as the Day of Descent, those who were born on the same day as the Day of Ascent, and others—i.e. those born on five other days. For example, if in a particular year the Day of Descent fell on a Tuesday and the Day of Ascent on a Thursday, the three classes would be 'Tuesday-borns', 'Thursday-borns', and others. People who fell in the first category were considered likely to meet misfortune during the course of the New Year unless they performed the hair-washing ceremony, and they had to perform that ceremony on the Day of Sojourn, which meant that if there were two Days of Sojourn they had to perform the ceremony on both days. People who fell in the second category were believed to be of good fortune for the coming year, but their good fortune would be greater if they performed the hair-washing ceremony. Such persons were known as 'Time's-Eaters', or 'Time's Servicemen', in the same way as the King's Servicemen were known as 'King's Eaters' because they were 'Eaters of the King's Rice', i.e. living on the salary granted by the King. These Time's-Eaters performed the hair-washing ceremony on the Day of Ascent. People in the third category were considered likely to have neutral luck (neither good nor bad luck) for the New Year, but their luck would be good if they performed the hair-washing ceremony, which had to be done on the Day of Descent. Thus the third category of people performed the ceremony on the first day, the second category on the last day, and the first category on the middle days of the feast. For the Burmese King the ceremony of hair-washing was one of the most important in the palace calendar, and he drove out in state to the bank of a river or a lake and performed the ceremony. The importance of the hair-washing ceremony waned with the passing of the Burmese kingdom in 1886, and nowadays everyone performs the ceremony on the New Year's day.

Explanations of the visit

There is still remembered a centuries-old explanation of this annual visit of the Thagyamin, the King of the Gods. When this earth first came into being there was no life on it. Some Brahma gods, from their own abode, saw the newly-formed world and, coming down to inspect it, they found the soil so sweet-smelling that they ate one or two lumps. As the soil was so tasty also, they ate more and more, and suddenly found themselves losing their supernatural powers. They could no longer see their palaces in their own world far away, and they could no longer fly back to their own abode. But they went on eating the sweet-smelling soil. Soon the celestial rays of light from their bodies disappeared, and in the total darkness that followed they lamented and cried out in fear until the King of the Gods came down to console them. Then, at his intercession, the gods of the planets decided to make themselves visible from the earth, and so the sun, the moon, and other planets were seen on the horizon to the delight of the earth-bound gods. Then vegetation appeared, and animals appeared. The earth-bound gods were instructed and taught many things by the King of the Gods, who then went back to his own abode, promising to come again at the end of one year. Thus, the Thagyamin has been annually visiting this earth since that time. The story is based on the account of the genesis of the universe as given in the Buddhist scriptures, according to which this earth dissolved and then re-evolved, when it was peopled by luminous beings with supernatural powers; they lost their luminous rays and their supernatural powers on eating the sweet-smelling soil, and as they cried out in fear in the ensuing darkness, the planets appeared one by one.[1] In the account given in the scriptures, however, the Brahma gods did not come direct from their own abode, but they 'died' and were 're-born' as luminous beings on the

[1] *Digha-Nikaya*, translated by T. W. Rhys Davids and J. Estlin Carpenter, vol. iii, p. 84.

newly-formed earth and, moreover, the King of the Gods was not mentioned at all.

There exists another story which continues the above tale. Years passed and generation after generation of their descendants came and went. One day an old man, having the ability to fly in the air as the result of meditating and performing mental exercises, flew to the walls of the universe and learnt by heart all the rules of astrology written thereon. Flying back to this earth he watched the planets and knew that his death would take place in a few minutes. Desperately looking round he saw a young man and his wife walking along a forest path, but at that very moment a snake suddenly appeared and bit the young man so that the latter died. Swiftly approaching the dead young man he sucked out the snake-poison with his mouth, and turning to the distraught young woman he soothed her by telling her to wait near her husband until he came back with some medicine. He walked some distance along the forest path and then, by his supernatural powers, let his soul enter the young man's body even as his old body died. The young man's body with the old man's soul now stood up and, pretending not to know anything about the old man, said to the young wife, 'Beloved, I know I was bitten by a snake, and yet I do not die.'

'A kind old man sucked out the poison from your body,' explained the wife, 'then he went to fetch some medicine, and I was awaiting his return.'

'We must follow him and thank him,' said the young man.

He led his wife some distance along the forest path and soon reached the dead body of the old man. 'Poor old man,' sighed the young man, 'he died so that I might live.'

Cutting down some branches from the trees he built a funeral pyre and burnt the dead body of the old man.

The wife never guessed the truth regarding her husband. Settling down with his young wife in a nearby town he earned his living as an astrologer. His fame soon reached the four corners of the world and he came to be known as 'Kawar-lamaing' or 'the Light of Wisdom'.[1] When the King of the Gods came down to the earth for his annual visit he heard of the great astrological predictions of the Light of Wisdom and decided to go and play a prank on him. Assuming human form, he went to the front porch of the astrologer's house and sat on a stump of a tree, with one leg dangling and one leg folded. Then, placing the left hand on his hip, and the right hand across his mouth so as to hide his laughter, he asked, 'Great astrologer, this fellow, the King of the Gods, where is he now?'

The astrologer, without looking up, worked out some formulas and replied, 'He is not in the abode of the gods.'

'Then if he is not there, where can he be?'

The astrologer again worked out some formulas and replied, 'He is on this earth.'

'What is he doing?'

'He is sitting on a tree-stump with one leg dangling, the other leg folded, left hand on his hip and right hand across his mouth hiding his laughter.'

'How many miles is he from this house and in what direction?'

The astrologer worked out some more formulas and looked up in surprise and said, 'My science tells me he is here right in front of my house and so you are none other than the Thagyamin himself.'

The god admitted his identity and praised the astrologer for his wonderful knowledge of astrology.

The following year as the King of the Gods was making ready for his annual visit to the earth, the Red Brahma (or the Arthi Brahma) came and discussed an astrological matter. The King of the Gods held the view that although there were eight days in the planetary week,[2] for all other astrological

---

[1] It may mean, also, 'the Wisdom of the Farmers'.
[2] See Chapter 2.

purposes the number of days in a week should be taken as seven. The Red Brahma insisted, however, that for all astrological purposes the week must be considered to contain eight days. The King of the Gods and the Red Brahma nearly came to blows until both decided to refer the matter to the human astrologer, the Light of Wisdom, making a bet that the one who was proved to be right should cut off the head of the other. So both gods went before the astrologer and asked him to settle the dispute without fear or favour.

The astrologer sighed, and said, 'Great gods, can you not cancel your bet first?'

'We gods never go back on our word,' replied the gods indignantly.

'Then, I give you this my decision,' adjudged the astrologer. 'The contention of the King of the Gods is right, because it is clearly written on the walls of the universe that for all astrological calculations, a week has seven days.'

In the silence that followed the astrologer's words, the King of the Gods, with his thunderbolt, cut off the Red Brahma's head, and it rolled down on the ground. Swiftly picking up the Brahma's head the King of the Gods explained, 'Great astrologer, I had to cut off his head, because otherwise he would have lived on in shame as a god who dishonoured his bet, and for the same reason I cannot put his head back on his body. On the other hand, I cannot let him die. Moreover, I cannot leave his head on this earth, because if I do so, it will burn up all living things and all vegetation in a few minutes; if I throw it into the sky, no rain will ever fall again, and if I throw it into the ocean, all the waters of the oceans, seas and rivers will dry up, for the head is burning hot and only a god can hold it.'

After some thought the King of the Gods gave his golden sword to the astrologer and instructed, 'Go at once towards due north and bring me the head of the first creature that you may find.'

The astrologer, taking the sword, ran swiftly towards due north and the first creature he happened to meet was an elephant which shone like gold. The astrologer cut off the head of the elephant and brought it to the King of the Gods who, placing it on the body of the dead Brahma, sprinkled some water on it, and lo, the Brahma was alive again with a red body and a golden elephant's head. As the Red Brahma he had a red and angry-looking face which frightened people away from him, but now, with a benign-looking golden elephant's head, he looked kindly and good-natured, and from that day onwards he was loved by human beings, who changed his name and called him Maha Peinne or 'the Great Delight'. As he was restored to life on this earth he now had a special regard for human beings, and since that day he has helped human beings to overcome difficulties and dangers and achieve their successes and victories. But the King of the Gods was still busy with the problem of the red head of the Brahma, and finally he called seven goddesses to come down to the earth, and he appointed them guardians of the red head; each was to carry the head in turn for a period of one year. Thus, at every Feast of the New Year, the goddess who has been carrying the head for the year which is ending passes on the head into the arms of the next goddess, who lifts up her hands to receive it. The time of the arrival of the Thagyamin coincides with the time when the goddess makes ready to pass on the head; the time of the Thagyamin's sojourn coincides with the time when the two goddesses are holding the head together, and the time of the Thagyamin's departure coincides with the moment when the first goddess lets go of the head, leaving it entirely in the care of the next goddess.

The above story has features which show that a Buddhist coating has been given to a Hindu original. It is obvious that the story originally was a creation myth, but in the new version, any reference to the universe having been created is carefully avoided. The Red Brahma is a Hindu and not a

Buddhist conception, because in the Buddhist modification of the Hindu world of gods, Brahmas are beings far superior to gods and do not interfere either in the affairs of gods or in the affairs of men, and the idea of a Brahma having a wager with the King of the Gods is alien to Buddhism. Also, in the popular Burmese world of gods and goddesses, the Brahmas are too pure and supramundane to take leading parts. The Red Brahma who changed into the God of the Great Delight is none other than the elephant-headed god of the Hindus, Ganesh.

In Hindu mythology there are four versions explaining how this god Ganesh, the son of Siva himself, came to be with an elephant's head. According to one version Saturn, or the god of the Saturday planet, came too closely and looked at the newly-born god and the glare from Saturn's face was so bright that the head of the new-born god shrivelled into nothing. According to another version, the newly-born god was so beautiful that a jealous goddess by a great curse shrivelled the head of the god into nothing. In the third version, the god's head was cut off by Siva himself, not knowing that the fierce god who was guarding his consort Chandi's bed-chamber was his and her own son. In the fourth version, the head of the god was cut off by demons in a great battle. Curiously enough, the Burmese version is not known in India. Ganesh was never mentioned in the earlier Burmese chronicles, unlike Vishnu, but a few of his images have been found at Pagan in recent excavations. At the present time, next to Vishnu, Ganesh is the most popular among the few Hindu gods worshipped as Burmese gods.

The idea of a soul being transferred from one body to another is again alien to Buddhism, which does not recognize the existence of a soul, but Burmese magical beliefs before Buddhism no doubt would have considered such a transfer possible, for even at the present day, Burmese magic and witchcraft recognize the possibility of a dead body being

made to seem to come to life again by an evil spirit entering it.
For example, it is believed that unless offerings have been
made to the guardian-god of the forest or unless some magical
charms are carried, a huntsman will often find the deer that
he has killed and whose head he has cut off, get up and prance
away.

The Thagyamin, the King of the Gods, is none other than
Sakra. In Hinduism he was Indra, the god of the thunderbolt, but he was adopted by Buddhism as its guardian-god
under the name of Sakra. When Prince Siddhata, the future
Buddha, after renouncing his family and his kingdom, cut off
his hair to become an ascetic, Sakra received the hair in a
golden bowl, and taking it to the abode of the gods he built
a pagoda over it. According to Mahavamsa, the standard
chronicle of Ceylon, he was charged by the Buddha to see to
the establishment of Buddhism in Ceylon and to act as its
special guardian there. According to a Burmese belief, when
the Buddha was nearing his death he thought of ordaining
that his religion should last 2,500 years, but Sakra begged
him to increase the period to 5,000, promising to guard it with
his thunderbolt during the second 2,500 years. Although
this Burmese legend is not found either in the Pali Canon
or the Commentaries, many Burmese still insist on referring
to the present era of Buddhism as 'Thagya's Era of
Buddhism'.[1]

The early chronicles mention that Sakra acted as one of the
seven celestial builders of the city of Prome, because Buddhism was destined to flourish in the Pyu kingdom, and that he
specially assisted Anawrahta's father to gain the throne of
Pagan, as Buddhism was destined to flourish in the new
Burmese kingdom. When Anawrahta had succeeded his
father on the throne further help from Sakra was unnecessary,
because Anawrahta had received from his father the Lance

---

[1] The 2,500th Anniversary of the Buddha's death occurred in 1956, according to Burmese reckoning.

of Victory,[1] which the latter had obtained from Sakra. This Lance of Victory, wielded by Anawrahta, has become famous not only in Burmese legends and chronicles, but also in the legends and chronicles of the neighbouring countries. For example, the Thai Chronicle of the Emerald Buddha mentions Anawrahta's coming to Thailand astride his flying Lance of Victory. Thagyamin was also mentioned in the chronicles as assisting in the building of the Shwezigone Pagoda and other famous pagodas at Pagan.

The name 'Thagyamin' means 'the Lord who knows and hears everything', and a twelfth-century fresco depicts him with two pairs of eyes, two pairs of ears, and two noses. 'Thagyamin', of course, may be just a Burmese derivative of the name Sakra; all the same, the Burmese belief that the god records the names of good and bad people in his Golden Book and Dog-Skin Book respectively, fits in with the title, 'the Lord who knows and hears everything'. That Sakra keeps a record of good deeds done by men is found in the Pali Commentaries, but the details of how this record is kept differ very widely from the Burmese legend; the Four Guardian Gods of the Earth and their followers visit the earth on every Sabbath day and they write down in a golden book the good deeds done by human beings, and they later hand the golden book to Sakra's musician, who in turn gives it to Sakra's charioteer, who submits it to Sakra; Sakra then reads out the details of the good deeds to the assembly of gods, who rejoice and say *Thar-du*, meaning 'good', 'well-done', 'wonderful'. It may be noted that the Commentaries make no mention of a Dog-Skin Book for evil-doers.

The Feast of the Thingyan

The Feast of the New Year is also known to the Burmese as the Feast of the Thingyan. The word 'Thingyan' is derived from a Sanskrit word meaning the entry of the Sun to any of

---

[1] It was also known as the Lance of Punishment.

the Twelve Signs of the Zodiac; the Feast of the Thingyan is called in Burmese astrology the Feast of the Great Thingyan, because it marks the movement of the Sun from the Sign of Pisces or the Fishes to the Sign of Aries or the Ram and it therefore marks the end of one solar year and the beginning of another. In the Burmese calendar, which is a lunar calendar, it is a movable feast, but it is fixable in the solar year, which explains the fact that whereas it falls on different Burmese dates in different years, it falls usually during the period 13th to 15th April and very occasionally during the period 13th to 16th April or 14th to 16th April in the western solar calendar.

It may be mentioned that in computing the year the Burmese do take into consideration the movement of the Sun, so that *Ta-goo*, the first month of the Burmese calendar, becomes divided into two parts, the first half belonging to the old year, the second to the New Year, and with the names 'Old *Ta-goo*' and 'New *Ta-goo*'. The Burmese make the adjustments between the lunar and the solar calendars by the introduction of leap years containing an intercalary *Waso*, the fourth month of the year, calling the regular month the First *Waso* and the additional month the Second *Waso*.[1] The time of the arrival of the Thagyamin is the time when the Sun moves out of Pisces, the period covered by the days of his sojourn is the time when the Sun is passing through a sort of no-man's-land between the two Signs, and the time of his departure is the time when the Sun enters Aries. In contrast to the Burmese, who begin their New Year from the time when the Sun completely enters the Sign of Aries, the Tamil Hindus and the Sinhalese mark their New Year from the moment the Sun moves out from the Sign of Pisces.

From these facts it can be clearly seen that the original purpose of the Feast of the New Year, like the Hindu

---

[1] I have given only the basic principle of the adjustments. The details are more complicated. For example, some leap years have, in addition to the intercalary month, an intercalary day.

Festival of Holi, the Chinese Festival of Ching Ming and the pre-Christian Festival of Easter, was to celebrate the vernal equinox, but owing to the precession of the equinoxes the feast and the equinox no longer coincide. In Burma, as in the case of the other countries of south-east Asia, the heat of the sun does not fluctuate much during the course of the year and there is no winter, and for that reason, perhaps, there seem to have been no Burmese feasts of midwinter, mid-summer and autumnal equinox. However, the spring equinox was celebrated, because it more or less heralded the coming of the rains.

The Burmese seem to have in primitive times two festivals to celebrate their three seasons, namely the Festival of the Vernal Equinox, marking the approaching end[1] of the hot season and approaching beginning of the rainy season, and secondly the Festival of the Lights in November, marking the end of the rainy season and the beginning of the cool season. In my opinion, the merry-making and the boisterous throwing of water during the Feast of the New Year at the present day originally belonged to that primitive seasonal Feast of the Vernal Equinox, and the magical purpose behind them was very probably to make rain. I do not think that the throwing of water was originally a purification ceremony because of the horseplay and merry-making that accompanied the water-throwing.

On the primitive feast of the equinox was later grafted the ceremony of the worship of the Sunday planet. The broad-sheets issued by the astrologers annually (issued under the authority of the king before 1886 and now issued by the Guild of Astrologers) are really almanacs giving general pre-dictions for the year; in these, the god who descends and ascends during the Thingyan period is definitely stated to be the god of the Sunday planet, and the colour of his dress, the

---

[1] 'Approaching', because the monsoon will break only some three weeks later.

implements of war or agriculture that he carries, and the animal he rides indicate the general characteristics of the year. Thus, if the god wears a reddish-gold dress, carries in one hand a king's sword and in another a sickle, and rides on the proper vehicle of the Sun planet, namely the *galon* bird, the year will be a normal year, neither too fortunate nor too unfortunate. If he wears a dress of gold, carries in one hand a bunch of flowers and in the other hand a pot of drinking water, and rides on a bull or a buffalo, the year will be an unusually peaceful and prosperous one. If he wears a flaming red dress, carries a burning torch in one hand and a spear or a broad sword or a battle-axe in the other, and rides on a *Naga* dragon or an ogre, the year will be full of bloodshed and disaster.

The most important part of the ceremony of the worship of the Sunday planet was the purification ceremony of washing the hair. The Chronicles mention that the king publicly performed the ceremony of hair-washing at the time of the coronation and at the feast of every New Year, and a less elaborate and private ceremony of hair-washing was performed at the time of the other eleven Thingyans when the Sun entered in turn the remaining signs of the Zodiac. The custom of setting free live fishes had a reference to the fact that the Sun had left the Sign of the Fishes, but when Buddhism became the official religion of the country this custom came to have a Buddhist flavour. In addition, the customs of keeping the sabbath, offering alms-food to the monks, and visiting the elders with offerings and gifts were also introduced. Above all, the Thingyan-Min or the God of the Thingyan, namely the Sunday planet, suddenly changed into Thagya-Min the guardian God of Buddhism, the Lord Sakra.

APPENDIX

The Feast of the New Year in Thailand

It may be mentioned that according to the Chronicles the Pyus used the Buddhist era, but abandoned it in favour of their own Pyu era in A.D. 78, and the Burmese at Pagan first used the Pyu era but abandoned it in favour of a new era, known as the Pagan or Burmese era, in A.D. 638. After Anawrahta had come to the throne of Pagan in A.D. 1044, the Burmese became the dominant race in the Indo-Chinese Peninsula and, after 1056, Pagan became the new centre of Buddhism. As a result, the Burmese era and the Burmese calendar were introduced to other countries in the region. It is not surprising, therefore, that the people of Laos celebrate their New Year exactly in the same way as the Burmese do and they have the same Burmese legend, customs and beliefs regarding the New Year. In Thailand, also, the New Year is celebrated in the same Burmese way[1] and the Thais call the feast the Songkran Feast, and Songkran is the Thai variant of the Burmese term 'Thingyan'.

However, there have been certain modifications in the intervening centuries. According to the Thai version of the New Year legend a young wise man was set some riddles by the Red God, and the wager was to cut off the head of the loser. At first the young man could not solve the riddles, but he discovered the solutions by listening to the conversation of some eagles. So the god lost the wager and in shame cut off his own head. The god's seven daughters were charged with the task of keeping the flaming head, and these goddesses took it to a cave in the abode of the gods. But, at the time of every New Year, one of the seven daughters takes the flaming

---

[1] In Laos and Thailand, the feast is an occasion for merry-making and horseplay. Fishes are also freed. But there is no throwing of water.

head from the cave and carries it in procession, attended by all gods and goddesses. After the procession is over the head is returned to the cave. Thus, the time of the Burmese 'descent' coincides with the time of the head being taken out of the cave, the Burmese period of 'sojourn' with the period of the procession, and the Burmese time of 'ascent' with the time of the head being put back in the cave.

Again, with the Thais, it is neither the King of the Gods nor the god of the Sunday planet who appears riding on an animal during the Songkran period: it is that goddess among the seven whose task is to take out the head and carry it in procession for that particular New Year. The Thai legend makes no mention of the Red God coming back to life with an elephant's head.

4

The Cult of Alchemy

The growth of alchemy

India seems to have been the first centre of alchemic experiments. From India, alchemy spread westwards to the Arabs, the Egyptians and the Greeks, later to the medieval Europeans, eastwards to Burma and farther east to China. By the fifth century A.D. alchemy was being practised in China and in Burma. The great period of alchemy in the world as a whole was roughly between the fifth century A.D. and the sixteenth century, when its popularity waned with the dawn of modern science. In Burma the great period of alchemy was roughly between the fifth century A.D. and the eleventh century, and it became almost a religious cult by itself. But in the eleventh century its popularity waned with the introduction of Buddhism into the country, for Buddhism frowned upon alchemy. Thus, after the eleventh century alchemy started to decay, and although the cult has never completely died out (even at the present day some indulge in alchemic experiments), it has long ceased to be in any way a rival to Buddhism.

The alchemist's goal

Alchemy in Burma is known as *Aggiya*, meaning 'the work with fire'. 'Work with fire' is indeed the essence of alchemy, for the alchemist endeavours to transmute metals by means of fire. This endeavour to transmute base metals into precious metals is not peculiar to the Burmese alchemist and was the common heritage of alchemists all over the world. But

Burmese alchemy has as its background a deeper philosophy— a philosophy so deep and developed at one time that it was almost a religion. The endeavour 'to turn lead into silver and brass into gold' is to the Burmese alchemist merely a first step towards a great goal, namely to discover by further experiment 'the stone of live metal', or 'the stone of live mercury', which is the Burmese equivalent of the Philosopher's Stone in European alchemy. Again, 'the stone of live metal' itself is not the final goal. The final goal is to attain, after more experiment, a superhuman body and an eternal youth.

After considerable effort the first stage is reached by the Burmese alchemist, when he is able to transmute base metals into precious metals. Using the results of the first stage of his experiments he continues with metals and metal compounds until he has evolved the 'stone of live metal'. The possessor of this stone can fly in the air, or dive not only under water, but underground. He cannot be wounded as long as he has this stone on his body, that is, in his mouth, under his hair-knot, in his hands, or under his armpits. He will be free from fatigue and disease. However, the body of the possessor of the stone is still just a human body, and the superhuman powers described above do not really belong to him but only to the stone, which by mere touch can turn 'lead into silver and brass into gold'. To obtain these powers, the possessor of the stone does not have to be the actual discoverer of the stone. Thus, when an alchemist has discovered the 'stone of live metal', he exposes himself to the danger of being robbed of it by evil spirits or jealous magicians. Burmese folklore is full of stories about this stone. The Chronicles mention the case of an Indian prince who came flying every day to the kingdom of Pagan from his kingdom in Bengal to pay court to a Burmese princess; he was not an alchemist, but he had somehow obtained possession of a 'stone of live metal', and with this stone in his mouth he was able to fly in the air.

The alchemist, however, does not rest on his laurels after obtaining the stone. He continues his experiments, using the stone. The aim of these experiments is to discover certain metal compounds which will make his body superhuman. The third stage is reached when the required metal compounds are evolved. In order to make his body superhuman the alchemist cannot just swallow these metal compounds as one swallows medicine. They must be absorbed in his body. For this, he must first swallow the compounds, when his body will become as if dead. Then he must remain buried in the earth for a full seven days. This 'temporary death' of his body will become permanent if he is exposed to the air during the seven-day period. Moreover, during this period he will be entirely helpless and at the mercy of his enemies, namely evil spirits and magicians. Evil spirits will be on the look-out for him out of sheer jealousy and malice, but the magicians wish to eat his body, not only because it is very tasty and smells like the choicest perfume, but also because by eating it, they will come to possess superhuman strength. The Chronicles mention two heroes of the kingdom of Thaton who acquired prodigious strength after they ate the body of an alchemist, which they were cooking for their master, a monk-magician.[1]

Therefore, when the alchemist has discovered the right metal compounds, the first task before him is to search for a faithful pupil who will bury him in the forest, away from human beings, who will scare away evil spirits and magicians, and who will watch over the spot under which the alchemist lies buried. When the faithful pupil has been found the alchemist makes him dig a hole in the ground and, on entering it, the alchemist will swallow the metal compounds. Then the hole is filled up, and seven days later the alchemist of his own accord and in great joy jumps out of it, for he has become a *Zawgyi*, a fully-developed alchemist. All the supernatural qualities of the 'stone of live metal' are now possessed by

[1] Details regarding these two heroes are given in Chapter 6.

him in his supernatural body. As he no longer needs the stone he gives it to his pupil as a reward for services rendered, and as a farewell gift. He will then enter the forest and come back to the abode of human beings very seldom, if at all. As the alchemist's body has become superhuman he can wander at will, flying in the air or travelling underground; physical fatigue is no longer known to him and his body needs no further nourishment. His body will remain youthful until he dies, and death will come to him only after thousands of years. In fact, before Buddhism, with its doctrine of the impermanence of all compounded things, influenced the Burmese mind, it was believed that the 'fully-developed alchemist' would live forever with his eternally youthful body. But even though Buddhism has influenced Burmese alchemic beliefs and the followers of the alchemic cult admit that death will come to all, including the 'successful' alchemist, they still maintain that when death comes to him, it will come without the decay and disease of his body.

The alchemist's philosophy

The above is a summary of the Burmese beliefs connected with alchemy. But what is the basic philosophy behind all these beliefs in the cult of alchemy? Burmese alchemy tries to solve the tragic problem of human life, why youth has to pass and man has to die. All men feel at one time or another the dark mood of despair when they say with Omar Khayyam,

> Alas, that Spring should vanish with the Rose,
> That Youth's sweet-scented Manuscript should close!

Burmese alchemy aims at achieving an eternally youthful body, and thus to create a beauty that never fades, and a youth that never dies.

But is the 'successful' alchemist happy after achieving his heart's desire? On the whole he is happy, but he also has his own troubles. His is an intensely lonely life. He does not have to eat, but occasionally he eats fruit, as he cannot eat meat because of its smell. Therefore, it follows that he cannot stay with human beings for more than a few minutes, as they are eaters of meat and smell too much for him. However, he is not a hermit or an ascetic, and in his youthful strength and vigour he does not have to mortify his flesh. Instead, he gives full play to his senses. He has endeavoured to obtain an eternally youthful body, so as to enjoy forever the pleasures of the flesh. He wants love, but as a human woman, being a meat-eater, smells too much, he cannot approach her and has to console himself with substitutes. On the slopes of the Himalayas there are trees whose fruits have exactly the size and shape of the average human maiden, and by his alchemic power the alchemist puts some sort of 'life' into them, so that the fruits become animated. He makes love to them with enthusiasm and zest, but unfortunately, as they are but fruit, they soon get crushed and become of no use to him. Moreover, this kind of fruit tree is not very common even on the slopes of the Himalayas, and so the alchemists are often fighting and quarrelling with each other as there are not enough fruit-maidens to go round.

But perhaps this belief regarding the fruit-maidens originated in the anti-alchemist propaganda which prevailed after the coming of Buddhism. The majority of the Burmese Buddhists frown upon alchemic experiments as a wanton waste of time, and look upon the alchemist as a seeker after gold and after sensual pleasures. In reply, those who still believe in alchemy will maintain that the alchemist wants to live for thousands of years, not because he wants the pleasures of youth, but because he wants to be alive when the next Buddha appears on this earth, so that he may worship him and attain the eternal bliss of *Nibbana*. To meet this defence, anti-alchemists will say that when the next Buddha appears after many thousands of years, the alchemist will have lost all sense of time and will be so busy quarrelling over his fruit-maidens that he will not remember to go and worship the Buddha. But all these arguments and counter-arguments seem to be afterthoughts, and the solitary but tranquil life of a *Zawgyi* must have appealed to many an ascetic and scholar. Thus, we find the great Burmese dramatist, U Kyin U[1] describing with sympathy and understanding this ideal of a *Zawgyi*:

At last I have achieved what I desired. I have obtained the 'stone of live metal', and I have also become a *Zawgyi*. My stone can turn lead into silver, brass into gold. I have eaten that compound of alchemy, which makes me above nature, above this earthliness. I cannot be hit by bullets and bombs, and swords and spears wound me not at all . . . I can be king. But what care I for worldly power? Make way, make way, I wish to leave the abode of human beings and retire to the forest.

I have reached a lovely part of the forest. Look at the flower-stems, look at the waterfall. Here is a streamlet, there is a little pond. Here pebbles, and silvery sand. Green moss covers that rock, green water flows silently down that stone. The heat of the noonday sun has no effect on the peaceful place. Short trees and tall trees, big trees and small trees, they stand side by side. This tree clings to its lover, that tree is defiant. This bush looks inviting, this bamboo looks charming. The place under that tree is smooth-lawned. Did some fairy play there before I came and disturbed and frightened it away? What a peaceful place! A poet can live here forever writing verses on this beauty![2]

The four elements

I shall now endeavour to explain the scientific theory behind Burmese alchemic experiments. The whole universe is believed to be made up of four basic elements, earth, fire, water, and air. Therefore, all things on earth, whether organic or mineral, also have these four elements. The human body,

---

[1] His literary career lasted from about 1819 to about 1850.
[2] Maung Htin Aung, *Burmese Drama.*

too, is made up of these elements. But behind these four elements there is an essential matter which is not subjected to decay or change. Things decay only because of the four elements, and if the essential matter can be purified of the four elements, it will be preserved from change and decay. The aim of alchemic experiments is to obtain that essence which is in all metals, and then introduce that essence into the human body, which will thus become free from the four elements, an immortal and eternally youthful body.

The nine metals

The Burmese alchemist knows nine metals and twelve metal compounds. The nine metals are classified as 'females' and the twelve metal compounds are classified as 'males'. The alchemist feels that just as in the universe 'perfection' can be obtained only through the union of female and male, so the essential matter in all metals can be obtained only through the union of female metals with male metal compounds. The following metals are used: lead, tin, antimony, zinc, copper, silver, gold, iron, mercury.

The first five metals are considered to be base metals, and the next two, silver and gold, are noble metals. The base metals can be transmuted into silver and gold. Iron and mercury are considered to be neither base nor noble. Therefore, to the alchemist, either iron or mercury must be the basic metal on which experiments with other metals will be made, and either in iron or in mercury the 'stone of live metal' will be obtained. Therefore, alchemists have been classified into two categories, 'those who work on iron' and 'those who work on mercury'. In the alchemy of all other countries mercury alone is considered to be the most important metal, but the Burmese consider iron to be as important as mercury in their alchemic experiments. The Burmese alchemists consider that there are one hundred and sixty-seven varieties of iron, and they are familiar with steel.

The twelve metal compounds

The following metal compounds are used: sulphur, alum, salt, nitrate, borax, sal ammoniac, camphor, lime, soda ash, arsenic, arsenic sulphide, mercuric sulphide. Sulphur is neither a metal nor a compound according to modern scientific terminology, and some of the above compounds are not metals at all. But the Burmese word *Dat* is a rather comprehensive term, and although the nearest English equivalent will be 'metal' it covers chemicals also.

The two lists given above do not contain any vegetable products, but Burmese alchemy also uses herbs and roots in the experiments with metals.

The Burmese alchemic code

The Burmese physician and craftsman are often accused of being very selfish persons who consider their knowledge and their experience to be 'trade secrets' and who therefore will not communicate their discoveries to others. The Burmese alchemist is also accused of the same fault. But the accusation is unfair. As in the case of the medieval European Trade Guilds, the Burmese physician, the Burmese alchemist and the Burmese craftsman will keep their 'art' secret from outsiders, but they will freely circulate their 'secrets' within their own professions.

With regard to the Burmese alchemist, there is a considerable body of literature on the subject of alchemy, but these writings are in code. Alchemists were never persecuted, as were the Ari monks, but the practice of alchemy was frowned upon by the new Buddhism of Anawrahta, and the alchemist became a social outcast. Therefore, after the eleventh century, the Burmese alchemists conducted their experiments in secret, but they communicated with each other regarding their experiments and discoveries. Many secret formulae were passed from hand to hand. Unfortunately, the alchemists could not organize themselves into a nation-wide group, and instead grouped themselves into different schools. Each school wrote down its discoveries in its own code. The code was a simple one, and the metals and metal compounds were given nicknames or secret names such as 'the lion', 'the tiger', 'the wife with many children', 'the wife with no children', 'the wife with many husbands', 'the mouse', 'the white cat'. The nicknames were used by all schools but applied to different metals. Thus, whereas one school would refer to gold as 'the big eagle', another would refer to it as 'the lion'. Therefore, by the fifteenth or sixteenth century, much of the energy of the Burmese alchemist was wasted in attempting to decipher the secret alchemic formulae.

The development of Burmese alchemy

One reason why alchemy flourished so much in Burma in the early centuries was the richness of the country in minerals, and all the 'metals' and 'metal compounds' were easily procurable in the country. All the same, alchemy has always been an expensive pursuit. Before Anawrahta, the kings themselves were patrons of alchemy, and Burmese folk tales tell of instances when royal treasuries became empty through kings financing alchemic experiments made by monks. Therefore, another reason for the decay of alchemy after the eleventh century was the withdrawal of royal patronage. Before the eleventh century the practising alchemists were generally Ari monks, but thereafter the practising alchemists were usually astrologers, physicians, gold and silversmiths, and scholars. These professional men were not very rich, and they endeavoured to make alchemy pay by using it in their professional work. Astrologers and physicians sold lumps of metal from their alchemic laboratories as charms and amulets, or positive cures for certain diseases. Scholars wrote plays, poems, and treatises on alchemy. Gold and silversmiths benefited directly from their knowledge of metals.

Some have regretted that whereas in Europe alchemy

developed into modern chemistry, in Burma alchemy has always been a superstitious practice. This view is not quite correct. Burmese alchemy did result in some important chemical discoveries, but Burmese chemistry was completely overwhelmed when Western chemistry suddenly came into the country after the British conquest. So the early Burmese alchemist was not a mere charlatan or an impostor. Of all the religious cults that existed in Burma before the advent of Buddhism, alchemy was the noblest, for Burmese alchemy aimed at a conquest of nature, and to discover for humanity a way to preserve the human body in its vigour and beauty.

5

The Cult of the Magus

It is not known whether there was a cult of the Magus in
Burma before A.D. 1056. However, the hero of Burmese alchemy, the monk Master Goat-Bull, seems to have been
worshipped as their patron by those interested in alchemy.
The following folk-tale gives the details of his life.

Why there are so many pagodas at Pagan

Long ago, when the people of Pagan were poor, there lived
a monk, who was an alchemist trying to discover the Philosopher's Stone. His alchemistic experiments were costly and
he had to rely on his patron, the king, for financial support.
The monk followed step by step the instructions given in an
old parchment book. The instructions were many and various,
and weeks and months passed. The royal treasury became
empty, and the people refused to pay any more taxes, saying
that the king was merely wasting his gold on an impostor.
The monk at last reached the final instruction: 'Then put the
lump of metal in acid, and it will at last be the Philosopher's
Stone'. He appeased the people with the promise that after
one more experiment the Stone would be ready, and the
people paid their taxes to the king. The monk put the lump
of metal, which was the result of all the earlier experiments,
in acid. Seven days elapsed, but the lump of metal remained
as before. The monk went to the king to acquaint him with
the fact that the experiment had failed. The people heard
that the experiment had failed and thought that the monk
had come to the king to ask for more gold, so they surrounded

the palace demanding that the monk be punished as an
impostor and a cheat. The king was in a quandary for he knew
that the monk was no impostor, but he did not know how to
pacify the people. The monk himself solved the problem by
putting his own eyes out. He then stood before the people and
said 'My sockets are now gaping, and do you not consider
that I am punished enough?' The people were satisfied that
justice had been done and ceased their clamour.

For days the monk sat in his laboratory in the anguish of disappointment. At last he felt so bitter against the science of
alchemy that he got up and broke all the jars and instruments.
Then he told the little novice, who had been his assistant in
all his experiments, to throw the useless lump of metal into
the latrine. The little novice did as he was ordered. At nightfall the novice noticed that the latrine seemed as if on fire
and he went running to the monk, shouting, 'Master,
master, look, the latrine must be full of fairies or ghosts!'

'Remember that I am blind,' replied the monk. 'Describe
to me the phenomenon.' When he had listened to the novice's
description the monk realized that the lump of metal had at
last become the Philosopher's Stone. He realized also that the
scribe who wrote the parchment book had written in mistake
'acid' for 'night-soil' (in Burmese 'Chin' for 'Chee').

The novice picked up the Philosopher's Stone and gave it
to his master. Then he was told by the monk to go to a meat-
stall and get the two eyes of a bull or a goat. But as it was
now late in the evening the meat had been sold out, and
only one goat's eye and one bull's eye remained. These
were bought and taken to the monastery by the little novice.
The monk put the two eyes above his empty sockets and
touched them with the Philosopher's Stone, and at once the
eyes entered the sockets. He recovered his full vision, although
one eye was big and one was small. 'I shall be known from
today as "Monk Goat-Bull",' said the monk jokingly to the
novice. Then he went to the king's palace and told the king of

his good fortune. He announced his intention of leaving the world of human beings the next morning and requested the king to melt all his lead and brass in huge pots in front of the palace at sunrise. 'You can tell your subjects to do likewise,' said the monk as he left the palace to return to his monastery. Although it was past midnight by this time the king sent his men to wake up the city by the sounding of gongs, and to tell the people that they should melt all their lead and brass in huge pots in front of their houses at sunrise. When the sun appeared Monk Goat-Bull came forth from his monastery, attended by the novice. He went first to the palace and then to all the houses, and threw his Philosopher's Stone into every pot. The Stone jumped back into his hand every time, its mere touch having turned the lead in the pots into silver and the brass to gold. The people of Pagan became very rich, and with so much gold and silver at their disposal they built the countless pagodas that still stand at Pagan today.

When he had passed every house, Monk Goat-Bull, still attended by his novice, went to Mount Popa. As the two stood at the foot of the hill the creepers from the mountain-side lowered themselves and gently lifted the master and pupil to the mountain-top. The monk dug up some magic roots and ground them with the Philosopher's Stone. The ground roots formed themselves into six medicine balls and the monk swallowed three. The other three he gave to the novice, who, however, could not put them in his mouth, for to him the roots looked like human flesh, and the juice from them looked like human blood. 'What ails you, pupil?' asked the monk. 'It is human flesh and human blood,' replied the novice with a sob. 'It is not,' said Monk Goat-Bull. 'Have I ever told an untruth?' But the novice was seized with nausea when he tried to swallow the medicine balls. 'It is clear that you are not fated to share my success in alchemy,' said the monk sadly, 'and we must say farewell here.' The novice bade a tearful farewell to his master, who gave him a piece of gold as a parting gift. The creepers then gently twined themselves around the novice and lowered him to the foot of the hill.

The novice felt lost in the world without his master and, instead of going back to the monastery, he went to his widowed mother. 'Mother, cook me my breakfast,' he asked. 'Son, you know that I am poor and I have no money to buy the rice,' replied the mother. The novice remembered the little gold piece his master had given him as a parting gift and, taking it out of his pocket, he gave it to his mother. When his mother was leaving the house he felt a gold piece in his pocket. 'Mother, mother,' he cried, 'did I give you the gold piece?' 'Here it is, my son,' replied the mother, showing the gold piece in her hand. The novice took out the other gold piece from his pocket and gave it to his mother. But when he again felt his pocket, there was another gold piece inside it. He took it out and gave it to his mother. But again there was a gold piece in his pocket. This went on until the mother had ten gold pieces in her hand, and still there was a gold piece in the novice's pocket. Then only did the novice realize that his beloved master Monk Goat-Bull had given him a perpetual gift of gold.[1]

The cult of the runes

The cult of magic and witchcraft originally included also the cult of the runes. The runes consisted of magical squares containing either letters of the Burmese alphabet or arithmetical figures, and it is believed that every potent rune is guarded by a guardian god. For reasons which are not known, the cult of the runes suddenly regained its popularity in the fifteenth century, when it took over many ideas from the cult of alchemy. Instead of experimenting in either iron or mercury, the follower of the cult of the runes experiments in casting square after square until he discovers the right squares. When he has discovered them he has to go through a final

[1] Maung Htin Aung, *Burmese Folk-Tales.*

process; either, like the alchemist, he is buried underground for seven days, or he is burnt in a fire for three nights. Then he emerges as a *Zawgyi* or 'a successful alchemist'.[1] When the cult regained its popularity in the fifteenth century it had disassociated itself entirely from the cult of magic and witchcraft and, in addition, it had hidden its origin under the cloak of devotion to Buddhism. This explains why a follower of this cult has now to keep the Eight or Ten Precepts and abstain from eating any meat while he is casting the runes. Usually he goes into retreat for a period of forty-nine days before casting a rune or a series of runes.

Dhamma-zedi

The most famous 'Master of Runes' in the fifteenth century was Dhamma-zedi. He and his companion, Dhammapala, were young Mons who entered the Buddhist order and settled at Ava, the new Burmese capital, after the fall of Pagan. It was in the third decade of the fifteenth century, when the kingdoms of Ava and Pegu had fought each other to a standstill. The two Mons were very learned in the scriptures and were also interested in the cult of the runes.

The king of Ava at that time had a Mon queen, the Lady Shin-Sawbu. She was the daughter of a very famous king of Pegu, Razadarit (A.D. 1385–1423), and had been married twice before, first to a previous king of Ava, and then, after his death, to a lord of Pagan, now deceased also. She was thirty-six and already a mother, but she still looked young and beautiful. However, she tired of life and informed the king of her desire to study the scriptures. The king appointed the two young Mon monks as her tutors, but after some months of study the queen and her tutors became conspirators, and one night in 1430 they fled down the river back to Pegu. She did not marry again and settled down to a life of

---

[1] So there came to be three kinds of *Zawgyis*, namely the Iron, the Mercury, and the Runes *Zawgyis*.

peace and tranquillity. But twenty-three years later, in 1453, she was elected queen of Pegu. She proved to be a great ruler until 1460, when she decided to become a religious recluse. She looked for a successor and decided that one of the two monks should take her place on the throne. However, as both were equally learned and able, and as both had been her benefactors, she could not make her choice between the two and decided to leave it to chance. So,

One morning when they came to receive the royal rice, she secreted in one of their bowls a *pahso* (layman's dress) together with little models of the five regalia; then, having prayed that the lot might fall on the worthier, she returned the bowls. Dhamma-zedi, to whom the fateful bowl fell, left the sacred order, received her daughter in marriage, and assumed the government. The other monk in his disappointment aroused suspicion and was executed at Paunglin, north of Rangoon.[1]

Dhamma-zedi proved himself to be not only one of the wisest of kings but also one of the greatest patrons of Budhism. But his interest in the runes remained undiminished, and on the great bell that still hangs on the platform of the Shwemawdaw Pagoda at Pegu can still be seen the runes that he cast and engraved thereon.

The above account of Dhamma-zedi is the dull and barren account given in the Chronicles and, according to the lore of believers in the power of the runes, there were certain details which the Chronicles refrained from mentioning. The beautiful queen and her two tutors were able to make the long journey by boat from Ava to Pegu without molestation because the two monks had cast a rune which changed the colour of the boat every day, so that the horsemen who chased the escaping queen along the river bank were never able to identify and recognize the boat correctly. After Dhamma-zedi had been chosen king, his companion, in great

[1] G. E. Harvey, *History of Burma*, p. 118.

anger and disappointment, cast rune after rune, which resulted in hundreds of demons entering the royal city. When people knelt in fear before them the demons shouted, 'We come because Shin-Sawbu cannot get a husband.' Dhamma-zedi cast some runes in return, and lo, the demons fell down lifeless and were found to be only wicker-baskets strung together. This went on every night until suddenly the wicker-demons ceased to appear. Dhamma-pala had discovered, by a supreme effort, the final runes and was now buried underground, watched by his faithful pupil some distance away. Dhamma-zedi guessed what was happening and caused a desperate search to be made. When the faithful pupil was found at last he was tortured until he revealed the place where his master lay buried. The place was hastily dug up by Dhamma-zedi himself, and it was just in time, because in a few moments the seven-day period would have been over. Even then, Dhamma-pala's lifeless body made a feeble attempt to lift the sword which was gripped in his hand. Dhamma-zedi, not being a magician, declined to eat the body of his former friend and companion and gave it an honourable burial. Many years later, Dhamma-zedi himself discovered the final runes and became a *Zawgyi* also. He is now regarded as the first patron of the cult of the runes.

Master Victory

The cult of the runes gained a second patron early in the nineteenth century, on the eve of the first war with the British. The new patron was Maung Aung or 'Master Victory', who may have been a contemporary historical personage, although the chronicles are silent about him. According to the lore of the cult, Master Victory was a young pupil in the monastery of his village, in the district of Prome, when an unusual incident took place. The presiding monk of the monastery came back from a period of retreat in the forest, looking haggard and carrying a book of brazen plates. He had an interesting story to tell. As he sat under a tree in the forest meditating, a person appeared in the gathering twilight, dressed in white and with a rosary hanging from his neck. Kneeling down, the man in white said, 'My Lord Monk, please help me to become a Master of Runes. All that you have to do is to hold these three runes for me as I make a great fire out of the twigs and branches. When the fire is ready I shall jump into it, and as I start to burn you must throw into the fire the first rune. Tomorrow, as darkness falls, you must throw the second rune into the fire and the next night you must throw the third rune into the fire. All sorts of strange and fearful and even pleasant incidents will take place during the three nights, but you are a monk, my Lord, and so threats and temptations cannot disturb you.'

The monk reluctantly agreed to hold the three runes and the man in white started to make the fire. When the fire was ready the man jumped into it, and the monk threw the first rune into the fire. At once the flame became as black as charcoal, thunder and lightning appeared in the sky, and hundreds of frightful-looking demons surrounded the monk shouting, 'Give us the runes, give us the runes.' The monk, however, stood firm until the thunder and lightning and the demons disappeared with the break of dawn, although the fire still burned black and fearful. Throughout the day there was peace in the forest, and with the approach of darkness the monk threw the second rune into the fire. At once the flame of the fire changed to a soft, silvery colour, sounds of sweet music were heard, and hundreds of goddesses surrounded the monk smiling, singing and dancing, and whispering at the same time, 'My Lord, we beg of you, please give us the rune.' The monk, however, stood firm, and the strange music and the goddesses vanished at dawn. Again there was peace and quiet in the forest, and at nightfall he threw into the fire the last rune. The flame of the fire now assumed the colour of pure gold, and the whole forest gleamed with a strange brightness.

Nothing untoward happened that night, and at dawn the next day, the man in white walked out of the fire, dressed in the costume of a *Zawgyi*. He said to the monk, 'Sir, you have helped me indeed and now, if you will enter the fire, I shall see that you emerge a *Zawgyi* also.' The monk, however, refused to accept the offer and the *Zawgyi* said to him, 'Sir Monk, as you do not care for riches or for power, all that I can give you as a token of my gratitude is this book of brazen plates on which I have written down the formulas of my runes.' After giving the book to the monk the Master of the Runes flew away and the monk returned to his monastery.

After narrating this strange story to his pupils the monk took to his bed and died soon after. As nobody dared to touch the brazen book, young Master Victory took it to his house and kept it there. Years later, Master Victory went to a university in India where he met two other Burmese students, one of them being the King's son himself. They became very fond of each other and after three years of study they returned to Burma. Master Victory now took out the book of brazen plates and carefully studied it. His companion at the university, the King's son, now succeeded to the throne as Bodaw-paya (A.D. 1782–1819). The third student became a monk, retired to a forest monastery and was never heard of again. Master Victory soon became famous as an expert in runes, until rumours reached the ears of King Bodaw-paya. It seemed that Master Victory was conspiring to seize the throne. The King sent his soldiers to arrest Master Victory. Soon they found him and, having tied him in chains, they put him at the bottom of their war boat and started to sail up-stream. To their surprise they saw Master Victory standing on the shore. The soldiers fell down on their knees and pleaded, 'Master, if you do not come with us we shall all be executed.' 'Send a report by a horseman to your King that you have captured me, and you may rest assured that I shall be lying in chains at the bottom of the boat the moment it arrives at the King's capital.' The soldiers sent the report as instructed, and when their boat reached the golden city some two weeks later they found Master Victory lying at the bottom of the boat tied in chains. The King summoned his subjects to the place of execution, and when all had come the executioners threw Master Victory into a deep ditch and buried him alive. That evening, as the King sat in full audience with his ministers, Master Victory appeared from nowhere. 'False friend,' said Master Victory to the King, 'did we not swear eternal friendship when we parted after our return from the university? You are indeed stupid to think that the Master of Runes would ever want your paltry little kingdom. Let alone killing me, try to rub out this "O" which I now write with chalk on your palace floor.' The King, in shame and in anger, rubbed out the 'O' but found to his chagrin two 'O's' instead of one. He went on rubbing out the 'O's' until the whole palace floor was covered with hundreds of 'O's'. Master Victory laughed loudly and said, 'Friend of my youth, with my runes I could have made you king of the whole world. But you have been faithless to me and now I shall say farewell to you for ever.' 'Master of Runes,' pleaded the King, realizing that he had been foolish, 'if you will not protect me, protect my grandson, the young Prince of Prome.' 'I shall do that,' replied the Master of Runes and vanished from view.

At the present day the majority of the devotees of the cult of runes no longer attempt to discover the secret of the potent squares, because they believe that there is no need to cast the runes themselves; provided they keep the Eight Precepts, go into retreat whenever possible, refrain from eating meat, and keep their faith in Dhamma-zedi and Grandfather Victory (Bobo Aung), one of the Masters will surely come and give them the runes, so that they will become *Zawgyis* and await the coming of the next Buddha. In other words, for them the cult of runes has become the cult of the Magus.

6

The Lord of the Great Mountain

The great mountain

Mount Popa is not very high. It is about three thousand
feet in height and it stands on a level plateau of some eight
hundred feet. The plain on which the plateau stands itself is
about a thousand feet above sea level. However, Mount Popa
seems to be a great mountain because it stands solitary,
almost in the centre of the plain of Myingyan. It has stood
sentinel over the varying fortunes of the Burmese people,
whose first settlements in the middle Irrawaddy valley were
in the Myingyan plain. It is an extinct volcano whose sub-
terranean fires first saw daylight some two hundred and fifty
thousand years ago, but whose raging fires died out only in
historic times. According to the Burmese Chronicles, in
442 B.C. there was a great earthquake and Mount Popa 'rose
like a cone from the plains'. There is a crater at the top of the
cone, but one side of the crater had been blown away during
one of the volcano's many eruptions. The crater is about a
mile in width and about two thousand feet deep. The presence
of volcanic ash makes the soil fertile, and the high ground
catches the moisture from the clouds. Therefore, while the
Myingyan plain itself is parched and bare of vegetation,
Mount Popa is covered by a green forest. Even nowadays
there are many flowering trees, though in ancient times the
slopes of the hill were wholly covered with flowering trees
which led to the hill being called 'Popa' which, in Sanskrit,
means 'Flowers'. Thus to the early Burmese it was the 'mountain of flowers', and it was also the 'great mountain', the
'golden mountain'.

Throughout human history people of all races have pictured their gods and goddesses as living on a mountain. The Buddhists believe that their gods and goddesses live on Mount Mayu, just as the Ancient Greeks believed that their gods and goddesses dwelt on Mount Olympus. In the same way, the early Burmese came to believe that Mount Popa was the home of their gods and goddesses. They came to believe, too, that beautiful ogresses, who lived not on flesh but on flowers, played hide-and-seek in the groves of Mount Popa, and that on its slopes there wandered magicians and alchemists in search of potent herbs and roots. In the flower-forests of the hill, moreover, there actually lurked robbers and outlaws. Anawrahta himself, while striving to regain his father's throne usurped by another, formed his army on the slopes of Mount Popa. Kyansittha, after the defeat of the forces of Anawrahta's son by the Peguan rebels, led the remnants of the Burmese army to Popa Hill to be re-equipped and reorganized. Perhaps at one time the hill itself was worshipped as separate from the gods and goddesses, and it was probably considered to be 'a hallowed ground of victory' whose very touch would give success to 'men of endeavour' in their 'mighty undertakings'.

The mighty men

'Mighty men of endeavour' were greatly feared by the king in the early periods of Burmese history because they were likely to seize the throne with the support of the people. On the other hand, if they were not too ambitious or mighty they would be given high posts in the king's army. One of the main aims of magic and alchemy, in fact, was the evolution of a body which was not only invulnerable but also prodigiously strong. The emphasis was not only on valour but also on physical might. Anawrahta himself had four famous generals in his army, three of whom were physically mighty, the first being a great swimmer, the second a great runner, and

the third a great climber. However, the fourth, the great
Kyansittha, was not exceptionally strong, but he was the
most skilful because he was the most intelligent. Anawrahta himself was not a mighty man and was always careful
to demonstrate that his superior intelligence and his
god-given lance were more powerful than unusual brute
strength.

The need for a new religion

The kingdom of Pagan was, in the beginning, merely a
cluster of nineteen villages. Under King Thinlikyaung, who
according to the Chronicles flourished in A.D. 344–387 but
who possibly reigned later than these dates, the villages felt
strong enough to form themselves into a city, and thus
Thiripyissaya came to be built on the bank of the river Irrawaddy. It was the forerunner of the city of Pagan. At that
time the religion of the people must have been very similar to
that form of animism now practised by the remoter hill
peoples of Burma. *Nat* spirits were worshipped everywhere in
the country but each village restricted its worship to its own
local *Nats*. It would seem that both the king and the people
were looking for a *Nat* which would be worshipped all over
the country, and which would become a national *Nat*, to be
distinguished from a local *Nat*. In other words, they were
looking for a new religion which would bind the various tribes
of the kingdom into a nation.

Mr. Handsome and Golden Face

At that time, according to the Chronicles, there was another kingdom to the north, the kingdom of Tagaung; here,
a great tragedy had occurred. On the outskirts of the city of
Tagaung there lived a mighty blacksmith, whose son became
even mightier. This son had a perfectly proportioned body
and came to be known as Mr. Handsome. Even as a young
boy Mr. Handsome was a great eater, but when he attained

full manhood it was said that he ate a quarter-basket of rice[1] at every meal. When he took over his father's smithy he wielded two hammers; with his right hand he held an iron hammer weighing fifty *viss*, and with his left hand he held another weighing twenty-five *viss*. When Mr. Handsome worked his smithy and when he used his hammers against the anvil, the whole city quaked and trembled. (It seems obvious that this account of Mr. Handsome preserves a memory of the various earthquakes in prehistoric and historic times which occurred in north Burma, especially when Popa was still active.) The news of this mighty man reached the king of Tagaung, who, fearing rebellion, ordered the arrest of Mr. Handsome. The blacksmith was warned in time and took to the forest.

The disappointed king now stooped to treachery. Now Mr. Handsome had a younger sister who was very beautiful. The king raised her to be his queen, and after some months told her, 'I no longer fear your brother because he is now my brother also. Invite him to Tagaung and I shall make him governor of the city.' The sister believed the king and sent messengers to Mr. Handsome, who came to Tagaung, unsuspectingly. But he was at once seized by the king's soldiers and tied to a *Saga*[2] tree on the bank of the Irrawaddy. The king, together with his queen and his court, now came on the scene, and he ordered that a huge fire be lit at the feet of the helpless blacksmith. As her brother writhed in agony in the fire the queen suddenly shook herself free from her maids-of-honour and rushed into the fire to die with him. The king, who had learnt to love her, tried to save her by pulling her back by the hair. But it was too late. Only her beautiful face was saved, as the rest of her body had burnt even in that short space of time. Later on, when she was worshipped as a *Nat* spirit, this was remembered and she was affectionately called 'Golden

---

[1] One basket of rice weighs about 70 lb.
[2] The Indian 'Champa' tree.

Face'. Thus the brother and sister died and they became *Nat* spirits and made their abode on the *Saga* tree. In their anger against the treacherous king the two spirits killed all the animals and human beings who came under the shade of the tree. The king was frightened and ordered that the tree be cut down and the trunk floated down the river. After some days the trunk of the *Saga* tree reached the new city of Thiripyissaya, where King Thinlikyaung and his people waited, for the account of the two *Nat* spirits had reached them. Here was the opportunity to establish a new religion or at least a new cult. The king's carvers soon carved out of the tree trunk images of the brother and sister, and then covered them with gold.

It was near the time of the full moon, and according to the English calendar it was December. The fields had been reaped, the harvest had been successfully gathered, and the people were in festive mood. The images of the two *Nats* were put on golden palanquins and attended by the king himself, they were carried along the road to Mount Popa. Red was the colour associated with *Nat* spirits and red flags and red streamers were carried by the people taking part in the procession and by the people who lived along the route. Everyone danced and sang, and when the procession halted at villages on the way, food and toddy-wine flowed free. The procession reached the summit of Mount Popa on the full moon day and a golden *Nat* shrine, newly constructed, awaited the two images. The images were set up in the shrine with great pomp and ceremony, and the king proclaimed that the village on the slope of the hill, Popa Ywa, was given as a perpetual fief to the two *Nat* spirits. As spirit mediums danced in abandoned joy, hundreds of white oxen, white horses, and white goats were sacrificed to the *Nat* spirits.

It was the ninth month of the Burmese year, and it seemed so propitious that the month associated with the magic number nine should now be associated with the two *Nats*.

Both were now given by the king the title of 'Lords of the Great Mountain'. The brother was given the title in a Burmese-Pali form, 'Min Maha-Giri'. (*Min* in Burmese means 'Lord', and *Maha-Giri* in Pali means 'Great Mountain'.) The sister was given a title in its pure Burmese form, 'Taunggyishin', *Taunggyi* meaning 'Great Mountain' and *Shin* meaning 'Lord'. However, the sister continued to be affectionately called 'Shwe-Myetnha', 'Golden Face'. The king further ordered that the month be renamed 'Nat-Taw', or 'the month of the Royal *Nats*', and fixed the full moon day in this month as the date of the annual festival in honour of the Popa *Nats*. The name of the eighth month of the Burmese year, Tazaung-mon, means 'the month of the Festival of Lights', and before the advent of the Lords of the Great Mountain the full moon day of this month was the occasion for the offering of lights to the gods of the planets in particular and to all gods in general. But the king now ordained that the festival of lights was to be held one month later, in the month of Nat-Taw.[1]

The worship of the Lords of the Great Mountain established as a national cult

The kings who followed Thinlikyaung on the throne of Pagan continued the royal patronage of the Maha-Giri spirits and the worship of these spirits became established as a national cult. When the city of Pagan was built in A.D. 849 the figures of the 'Brother and Sister' were carved on the pillars of the main gate, to symbolize the fact that they were the guardian *Nats* of the city and the people. Every king's first visit to the mountain was considered as important as his coronation, and as the date of his coronation was noted down carefully by palace officials, so the date of his 'climbing the Golden Mountain' was carefully recorded. The Lord of the Great Mountain was believed to make himself visible to each

---

[1] See the Appendix to this chapter.

reigning king of Pagan and to advise him on important state affairs. When a monk known as Popa Sawrahan, who had his monastery in the Popa region, became the king's chaplain and was later elected to succeed him, the Lord of the Great Mountain refused to make himself visible to the new king, since he was not of 'royal bone'. Some years later the king had a daughter born to him, and when she was of age he married her to the son of the former king and declared him as his heir.[1] Only then did the Lord of the Great Mountain appear and advise the king. This story, given in the Chronicles, might very well be a formalized or popularized account of an actual event; perhaps the king at first refused to recognize the worship of the Lord of the Great Mountain until he became interested in gods and planets and astrology, for he was the king who, a few months before he died, had established the Burmese era for astrological reasons, abandoning the Pyu era.

Byat-ta and Byat-wi

After Anawrahta came to the throne he was always slightly suspicious of the Popa region as a possible centre for the plotting of rebellions against him. After the fall of Thaton he appointed a 'mighty man of endeavour' to be his representative in the Popa region. This person was Byat-ta, who had a romantic career behind him, as the following account of his life will testify. One morning, a monk who lived on the Zingyaik Hill near the city of Thaton saw some unusual object floating on the sea at the foot of the hill.[2] He went down and found that it was a large wooden tray, to which were tied two infants. On the desolate shore and the desolate sea there was no other sign of life, and the monk guessed that the ship on which the two infants were travelling had been wrecked and that the parents had tied them to the tray and thrown it

[1] Tin & Luce, *The Glass Palace Chronicle*, p. 52.
[2] It is believed that the sea came right up to the foot of the Zingyaik Hill in those days; in any case Thaton was originally a seaport although it is now some miles away from the sea.

overboard so as to save them from drowning. On looking over the two children the monk discovered that they were both boys and they were Indians by race.[1] He took them to his monastery and, naming them Byat-wi and Byat-ta, he brought them up as his pupils. Years passed and the boys became fully grown young men. One day the monk found on the hill-side the body of an alchemist who had died during the final stages of his experiments, and he instructed his pupils to carry it to the monastery and roast it. After the body had been roasted the monk said, 'Look here, pupils, the roasted flesh of the alchemist is to be eaten only by the Great King of Thaton, so that he will become a mighty man of endeavour and protect our country from its enemies. So I must go to the city to invite the King to dinner, and while I am away be good boys and keep careful watch.'

The youths waited and waited until it was night. In the darkness the roasted body of the alchemist shone like gold, and it gave out such a sweet flavour that the two youths yearned to taste the strange flesh. They were just two hungry boys and knew nothing about alchemy or the magical qualities the flesh of an alchemist possessed. Nevertheless, they waited until midnight, when the elder said to the younger, 'Let us just take a bite each', and they cut off a tiny part of the roasted body and ate it, but as the flesh tasted so good they greedily went on eating until the whole body was finished. The younger brother wailed, 'Our teacher will beat us black and blue for disobeying him', but the elder brother was more reckless and he replied, 'Brother, do not worry about the future, but let us enjoy ourselves.' Then, feeling gay and strong, he lifted the monastery from its foundations and turned it upside down. 'Is that all you can do?' mocked the younger brother, and he lifted a huge rock and placed it on the path along which the monk had gone to the city. Then

[1] According to a tradition among spirit mediums the boys were Arab Muslims.

they spent the rest of the night wrestling and running races until the next day dawned. At sunrise they saw their teacher and the king coming up the hill. Losing courage, the two brothers ran down the opposite side of the hill and hid themselves in a ravine. The monk saw the huge rock and the upside-down monastery and realized that the worst had happened. 'Alas, Lord King,' he exclaimed, 'it was indeed unfortunate that affairs of state did not allow you to leave the city until this morning. I fear that my boys have eaten the roasted alchemist, and unless they are quickly apprehended they will rebel against you.' On reaching the hill-top the monk and the King looked for the youths everywhere but to no avail. Hurrying back to the city the King sent out his soldiers to search for the two young men, but as Byat-wi and Byat-ta had become so strong and so swift, the soldiers could not capture them.

The two brothers wandered from village to village robbing and stealing. After some months, on one moonlight night, the more reckless Byat-wi said, 'Brother, let us enter the Golden City and make fun of the King and his soldiers.' In spite of the younger brother's protests the elder brother jumped over the walls of the city, and the younger brother had no choice but to follow. Then they went all round the city robbing and stealing. The next night, again, the brothers entered the city, and the elder brother said, 'I will rob the governor of the city himself, because he is its military commander.' So he went to the governor's mansion and jumped on to the sill of a bedroom window. It happened that the bedroom was occupied by the governor's only daughter, Mistress Oza, and she woke up with a start. The two young people looked at each other and fell in love at first sight. 'My Lady Beautiful,' Byat-wi whispered, 'I am the elder of the two outlaws whom the governor of the city desires to capture. You can give the alarm and I will surrender, because I want to gaze on you for some more moments.' 'Bold Outlaw,' replied Mistress Oza, 'how can I betray you who admire my beauty so much? I am the governor's daughter, but I shall not give the alarm.' So they spent the night in sweet conversation until the approach of dawn, when Mistress Oza prevailed upon her lover to run away. The next night he came again, and after that, at irregular intervals, the two lovers met.

As time passed, the servant-maids in the governor's household discovered the liaison and reported the matter to their master the governor. Realizing the magical powers possessed by the outlaw, the governor consulted a master of magic as to how he should capture Byat-wi. 'Get the skirt of a woman who has died in travail,' advised the master of magic, 'and hang it above the bedroom window by which the outlaw usually enters.' So that night the governor hung up the skirt of a woman who had died in travail on the bedroom window and he waited with his soldiers behind some concealing bushes. However, the outlaw did not come because his younger brother had begged him not to go too often into the city. The governor continued his watch and, on the third night, his patience was rewarded. He saw the outlaw entering through the bedroom window, and surrounding the house with his soldiers he rushed into his daughter's bedchamber. The outlaw saw him coming and, unafraid and smiling, he jumped out of the window but, alas, his magical powers were now lost and he fell and lay helpless on the ground below. He was taken before the King and sentenced to death. But his body still remained invulnerable although no longer strong, and the clubs, the swords, the spears and the arrows of the executioners broke in pieces against his flesh. The King, in great anger, ordered him to be trampled to death by elephants, but the legs of the elephants broke and the young outlaw remained alive. After three days of such vain attempts to kill him Byat-wi became weary of life. So he said to the King, 'My Lord, as you desire my death so much, I am willing to die, but send your executioners away and ask my beloved to

70

come and give me a chew of betel and a cupful of water.'[1] The King decided to grant his request, and soon Mistress Oza came, weeping, and holding in one hand a chew of betel and in the other a cupful of water. Leisurely the outlaw chewed the betel, leisurely he drank the water. He gazed into his lover's face and died with a smile on his lips. On the advice of the master of magic the body was cut into pieces and some parts, together with the entrails, were buried under the throne-room of the King's palace. The blood from the body was sprinkled over the city wall, though the amount of blood obtained was not quite enough for the entire wall and a space 'just enough for a hen to lie down' was left unsprinkled.

A few days later, Anawrahta's army arrived and attacked the city, but even the commander, Kyansittha himself, was unable to scale the walls because of a single soldier of prodigious strength, who alone seemed to guard the walls. The younger outlaw, lurking outside the wall, was soon found by the Burmese and Kyansittha prevailed upon him to serve under him. That night Byat-ta went up the walls alone, and as the mighty enemy soldier rushed towards him he recognized that it was the ghost of his dead brother. 'Let me in, my poor brother,' pleaded Byat-ta to the ghost. 'Let me have our revenge on your murderers.' The ghost replied, 'Alas, brother! My blood is sprinkled over these walls and my entrails are buried under the throne-room. I am doomed for ever to serve the tyrant king, and deny entry to all his enemies.' 'How can I help you?' asked the younger outlaw. 'There must be a way to free your spirit from being earth-bound for ever.' The ghost remained silent for a while and then said, 'Brother, there is one spot on these walls which was not sprinkled with my blood. I will show you the place and if you can jump over the walls of that particular spot I

---

[1] The literal translation would be 'a fold of betel leaf and a coco-nut cup of water'. The folded betel leaf would contain some betel nuts, tobacco, and lime. A common drinking cup of the Burmese until modern times was a cup made out of a coco-nut shell.

am under no duty to hinder you. After that you can use your wits to give victory to the Burmese.'

Byat-ta reported the matter to his commander. The following night he led Kyansittha and a few chosen men to the unguarded spot on the walls and entered the city. They fought their way to the throne-room and dug up the entrails. The ghost suddenly disappeared from the walls and the rest of the Burmese army marched in. After the victory Byat-ta and Kyansittha threw the entrails into the sea.[1]

Anawrahta appreciated the services rendered to his cause by Byat-ta and, according to the Chronicles, he liked the young man's frank and simple ways. But both he and Kyansittha had to be careful of 'mighty men of endeavour' and perhaps that was the reason why Byat-ta was not appointed to the army. Of course, Kyansittha and the other commanders were also described as 'mighty men of endeavour', but Kyansittha's might was in his brains and the other three commanders claimed to possess only superhuman strength, not supernatural powers. Byat-ta's main duty after being appointed to the Popa region was to bring flowers fresh every morning to Anawrahta in time for the daily audience. As his body could move with magical swiftness he never rode on horseback, but ran the whole distance, some forty-six miles.

The offering of flowers as a gesture of submission is a very old Burmese practice. In any race a bunch of flowers was placed at the finishing post by all the contestants, and the rower, horseman, or runner who was able to seize the flowers first was the winner; in a boxing or a wrestling match, the second outside the ring could throw in a bunch of flowers as a token of surrender in the same way as his European counterpart throws in the towel. Even to the present day a Burmese child, when he is unable to solve a riddle set by his opponent,

---

[1] The above account of Byat-ta is based on oral tradition and late nineteenth-century Burmese plays. The Chronicles give only a bare outline of the story.

has to say, 'I offer you flowers', and the other child will then give the solution. Therefore it was both a ceremony and a ritual for ministers and courtiers to offer flowers to Ana-wrahta at each morning audience.

Byat-ta's daily duty had a double purpose; it provided the ministers and courtiers with flowers, but it was also symbolic of the homage owed by Byat-ta himself and the Popa region to the King. While gathering flowers one morning he met a 'Flower-Eating Ogress'. Falling in love at first sight with each other they agreed to marry. But this romantic encounter resulted in Byat-ta being late for the morning audience, and he was severely warned by the King. A year later a son was born, and again Byat-ta was late and again he was severely warned. Next year a second son was born, and Byat-ta was late as before, but this time Anawrahta ordered his immediate execution. Knowing that Byat-ta was reputed to be invulnerable, Anawrahta lent his 'Spear of Punishment' to the executioners, who, meeting Byat-ta on the road to Pagan, killed him with it. Anawrahta refused to take any advantage of the magical qualities of Byat-ta's dead body and ordered it to be burnt on a funeral pyre. Byat-ta's ogress wife died of a broken heart, and Anawrahta was seized with pity and he took the two young sons under royal patronage. They later became heroes and were also executed under Anawrahta's orders, and again with his god-given spear.[1] With the death of these two heroes the cult of magic and alchemy suffered a great set-back in the kingdom.

Anawrahta tries to suppress Nat-worship

By the time Anawrahta came to the throne various local *Nats* had crystallized into a pantheon of thirty-six national *Nats*, with Maha-Giri as the head. They were the Thirty-six Lords worshipped by the people in the kingdom. Of all the pre-Buddhist cults that existed in the kingdom, Anawrahta

[1] Further details of these two brothers are given in the next chapter.

found this the most difficult to suppress. At first he tried to suppress spirit-worship altogether. He ordered the seizure of all images of the planet and Hindu gods and put them in a Vishnu temple, which was renamed 'Nat-hlaung Kyaung' or 'the Monastery where all the *Nats* are kept prisoner'. The temple still stands at the present day. Then he turned his attention to the cult of the Thirty-six *Nats*. To show that the *Nats* were not so powerful as himself he went about the city and the kingdom pulling down *Nat* shrines and beating the images with the flat of his spear. Even during his Chinese campaign he beat the copper image of Sanni, the ancestral god of the king of what is now Yunnan, and it was said that the image cried out in fear and pain. But he found that the cult of the Thirty-six Lords was too firmly embedded in the minds of the people for him to suppress entirely. One main reason for the popularity of the worship of the 'Lord of the Great Mountain' and the other Lords was the appeal of its ritual music and dancing. Even at the present day, during a spirit festival, the musicians play and the spirit mediums dance with such abandoned joy that even the most cynical onlooker often finds himself beating time with his hands or his feet to the primitive and sometimes even wild tunes of the mediums.

He finally allows it to survive with modifications

When Anawrahta frowned on the cult of the Thirty-six *Nats* worshippers stayed away from the shrines, and the spirit mediums, out of economic necessity, became strolling musicians and players, touring the countryside. And as their fear of the Thirty-six Lords was greater than their fear of Anawrahta, they always began their performances with a ritual offering of fruit to the Lords, accompanied by a short ritual dance and song.[1] Finally, Anawrahta permitted the

---

[1] Even now, at the beginning of every musical or dramatic show, an offering is made to the Thirty-seven *Nats*. This practice is followed not only by professional dancers, musicians, and actors but also by amateurs.

cult to survive, but only after modifications, so as to make it subsidiary to the new faith. He changed the number of spirits from thirty-six to thirty-seven by adding to the list Thagya-min,[1] the king of the Buddhist gods and the guardian god of Buddhism. Thagyamin was made the head of the pantheon, thus replacing Maha-Giri. Anawrahta also set up images of the thirty-seven *Nats* on the platform of the Shwezigone Pagoda that he built, saying, 'Let the people come to worship their old gods, and then they will discover the truth of the new faith of Buddhism.' The images were depicted in an attitude of worship, and the thirty-seven *Nats*, therefore, were shown to be supporters of the new faith, like many other gods and goddesses guarding the great pagoda. In addition, he replaced two *Nats* on the list by the *Nat*-spirits of two of his heroes (Byat-ta's sons) whom he had executed. This cult of the thirty-seven *Nats* has survived up to the present day, al-though from time to time a few of the less important *Nats* in the list were replaced by new *Nats*. Anawrahta strictly pro-hibited the sacrifice of animals at the annual festival on Mount Popa, and withdrew royal patronage from the festival. He also permitted the establishment of a rival festival at Taung-byon village, north of modern Mandalay, in honour of his two heroes, Byat-ta's sons.

Kyansittha's conciliatory policy

Anawrahta's son Saw Lu, who followed him on the throne, reigned only for a short period. He was involved in a bitter struggle against the rebellious governor of Pegu, and there-fore there was no time for the continuation, or otherwise, of Anawrahta's religious policy. But Saw Lu's immediate successors, Kyansittha and Alaungsithu, although they were great patrons of Buddhism and contributed greatly to the further propagation of the new faith, became closely associ-ated with the revival of the cult of the Popa *Nats*.

[1] The Thagyamin has been described in Chapter 3.

Kyansittha, after suppressing the Pegu rebellion, followed a policy of conciliation, in contrast to the stern discipline of Anawrahta. Anawrahta, in his threefold task of uniting a medley of tribes into a nation, of bringing under one rule the whole geographical unit of Burma, and of replacing primitive cults by Buddhism, had to exercise a discipline which was uncompromising, harsh and impatient. But by Kyansittha's time, the seeds sown by Anawrahta had developed into ripened grain, and Kyansittha reaped the harvest by gentler methods. From the account of his coronation, given in the contemporary inscriptions at the pagodas he built, we know that Kyansittha appreciated the Burmese love of feasting and merry-making, and all festivals were allowed to be held provided they were given a Buddhistic colouring and provided they did not revive the more primitive and barbarous practices which used to be connected with them before. Although he himself did not give his patronage to the revival of the cult of the planets and the Hindu gods, he brought this cult under royal control by insisting that he was the re-incarnation of Vishnu himself, and had taken part in the building of Prome. He himself was eager to restore royal patronage to the cult of Maha-Giri, but he was careful that Maha-Giri should play the role of a guardian-god of Buddhism, in addition to his ancient role of the guardian-god of the King and his peoples. But once royal patronage had been restored he could merely turn a blind eye to the surreptitious revival of animal sacrifices at the annual Popa festival. His successors to the Burmese throne could not suppress it until the coming of Bayinnaung, some five hundred years later. In one stroke he ended, for ever, the barbarous practice.

Kyansittha and the Monk of Popa

Kyansittha probably had a personal reason for restoring royal patronage to the cult. While regrouping the Burmese army in the woods and ravines of Mount Popa after the

defeat inflicted on Saw Lu by the Governor of Pegu, Kyansittha was assisted and advised by a strange and mysterious
personage, the 'Monk of Popa', or 'Shin Popa'. He was, perhaps, a Buddhist monk, although he continued the tradition
set by the Ari monks of practising magic and alchemy; or,
probably, he was an Ari monk, who was not persecuted as he
supported the new faith. (He should be distinguished from
the 'Popa Saw Rahan', 'Lord Monk of Popa', who became
king of Pagan in A.D. 613, and who has already been mentioned above.) This new Monk of Popa performed magical
rites so as to ensure victory to the defeated army, and his
prestige greatly increased when victory actually came and
Kyansittha became king of Pagan. Just as Kyansittha had
brought the revived Vishnu cult under royal control by
maintaining that he himself was a reincarnation of Vishnu,
he now brought the cult of Min Maha-Giri under royal
control, by announcing that Shin Arahan the Primate, the
Nat, and he were companions in arms in a previous existence,
and that Min Maha-Giri had been assisting him to gain the
throne of Pagan and act as the great Patron of Buddhism.
I quote from the *Glass Palace Chronicle*:

Likewise the Maha-Giri spirit showed himself and forbade the
King. Then said King Htihlaingshin,[1] 'If the Maha-Giri spirit
prayed with me of yore, why helped he me not when I was in
misery?' And the Maha-Giri spirit answered: 'O King, when
Anawrahtaminsaw tied thee with a rope and thrust at thee with
his spear, and by my help the blow fell on the rope that bound thee
and it snapped and thou, O King, went free, who helped thee but
I?' 'True!' said Htihlaing Kyansittha, 'I knew not that the spirit
helped me.' Said the Maha-Giri spirit: 'When the battle brake in
Taunghkwin and thou, O King, didst flee in the darkness of the
night, who but I went before thee on a striped horse, dressed in a
monitor skin, and shewed thee the way?' 'True!' said the King, 'I
knew not that it was the spirit.' Said the Maha-Giri spirit: 'When

[1] He was the Lord of Htihlaing Village before he became King.

thou stolest Sawlu and men pursued thee, and thou wast aweary
and couldst swim no longer, who but I created an islet and cried
like the *myittwe* bird? Who but I, in the guise of fishermen, father
and son, conveyed thee to the farther bank of Aungtha in a small
tanswek boat?' 'True!' said the King, 'I knew not that it was the
spirit.'[1]

The Lord of the Great Mountain within the House

Nowadays Min Maha-Giri is known as 'Eindwin-Min Maha-
giri', meaning 'the Lord of the Great Mountain, who is also
within the House'. In every Burmese village home, if no
longer in the cities, a coco-nut is hung at the top of a house-
post in an inner room. The coco-nut is covered with sandal-
wood and perfume, and a red cloth shaped like the head-
dress (*gaung-baung*) of a Burmese male is tied around it.
The coco-nut is an offering to the 'Lord of the Great Mountain', and it is associated with the *Nat* for two reasons.
Firstly, coco-nuts, bananas, and plums are fruits usually
offered to the Hindu gods and the thirty-seven *Nats* and
secondly, the milk from the coco-nut is given to a person
suffering from burns or high fever, as it is believed that coco-
nut-milk will bring relief to the patient.

The fact that Maha-Giri as Mr. Handsome was burnt to
death is never forgotten. Just as a coco-nut is acceptable to
the *Nat*, so a *Saga* flower is not acceptable, as Mr. Handsome
was tied to a *Saga* tree when he was burnt to death, and so,
when flowers are offered to the *Nat*, the *Saga* flower is always
left out.

But how has the 'Lord of the Great Mountain' become the
guardian *Nat* of every Burmese household? The Burmese,
before Anawrahta, worshipped a spirit who was known as the
'House-Guardian'. A little shrine was built in front of the
house and offerings of fruit and flowers were made every day
to the House-Guardian. According to a Burmese law tale, a

[1] Tin & Luce, op. cit., p. 107.

man had to cut down some trees to build his house and, as a result, the spirit living in a tree found himself without an abode. The spirit sued the man for compensation, and the court ordered that an artificial tree, namely a wooden shrine, be built in the compound of the house and the spirit was to dwell there, receiving regular gifts of fruit and flowers. It is not known whether this tale explains the origin of the cult of the House-Guardian, but it is definite that the cult is very old and was known not only to the Burmese, but also to the Mons and Khmers. To the present day the cult exists in Thailand. Even in the city of Bangkok there is a little shrine in every house, but unlike that of the ancient Burmese, the shrine is a little distance away from the house, although it is in the compound of the house itself. When Anawrahta destroyed the public *Nat* shrines, the people in fear destroyed their own private shrines dedicated to the worship of the House-Guardian. But, in secret, devotees went on offering red cloth, fruits and flowers to the Lord of the Great Mountain and fruits and flowers to the House-Guardian. But as there were no shrines now, the offerings meant for the Lord of the Great Mountain were made to the House-Post in the front room and the offerings meant for the House-Guardian were made to the House-Post in the bedroom. However, as Anawrahta's persecution of spirit worship became fiercer, more care had to be exercised, and the devotees restricted themselves to the offer of a single piece of red cloth to the Lord of the Great Mountain and a single coco-nut to both the Lord of the Great Mountain and the House-Guardian. They made the offerings to the House-Post in the bedroom. In course of time the different personalities of the two gods became merged into one, namely 'the Lord of the Great Mountain who is within the House'.

APPENDIX

The Festival of Lights

The Burmese Festival of Lights was originally held in the eighth month of the Burmese year, namely Tazaung-mon. The Feast of the Full Moon of Tazaung-mon was celebrated in three ways. First, the villagers danced, dressed as animals, some of which were from native mythology. Second, oil-lamps and wax-candles were lighted along the streets and in the houses of the villagers as offerings to gods in general. Third, at night there was a Feast of Fools, in which young men roamed the village, throwing *Zipyu* fruit at the houses and stealing articles which would cause inconvenience to the owners, or amusement to the onlookers, when they were found displayed at inappropriate places next morning. For example a woman's under-skirt would be flying from a pole in front of the headman's house, or a great number of cooking utensils would be found in a heap in the market-place.

Like the pre-Buddhist Feast of the New Year, the pre-Buddhist Feast of Tazaung-mon was a boisterous and rowdy one. After the cult of the Lord of the Great Mountain was established, the Festival of Lights was transferred by royal decree to the following month of Nat-Taw. The Festival of Tazaung-mon was no longer celebrated with lights, but it remained an important festival. As Anawrahta discouraged and belittled the worship of the Lord of the Great Mountain, the Full Moon of the seventh month, Thadingyut, became the occasion for the new Festival of Lights. This celebrated the end of the Buddhist Lent and also commemorated an event in the Buddha's life, namely, the return of the Buddha from the abode of the gods, where he had spent the previous Lent preaching to the gods. The lights were no longer offerings to gods in general or to the Lord of the Great Mountain, but to the Buddha. But, in secret, some meant them as offerings to the Lord of the Great Mountain, and as centuries passed there evolved a compromise. In time the festival became lengthened to three days, namely, the day before the Full Moon, the Full Moon day itself, and the day after. On the third day, in addition to the many lights lit in worship of the Buddha, a light each was lit in the inner room of a house, on the stairs and in the kitchen, in honour of the House-Guardian, namely the Lord of the Great Mountain. This is the practice that prevails up to the present day.

The Full Moon of Tazaung-mon is still celebrated in Upper and Middle Burma with animal dances and rowdyism, merry-making and thieving for fun, but since Anawrahta's time, no lights are lit. In Lower Burma, however, Tazaung-mon is still celebrated as the Festival of Lights. It is celebrated as a purely Buddhist festival, but no Buddhistic explanation is attached to it. Some scholars have attempted to show that in the eighteenth and nineteenth centuries the Burmese kings held Palace Festivals of Lights in honour of the Gods of Mount Mayyu[1] on the Full Moon day of Tazaung-mon, and that the people imitated this new Palace custom, which resulted in another Buddhist Festival of Lights in Tazaung-mon. It is difficult to accept this theory in view of the fact that no festival of lights in Tazaung-mon is held in Upper Burma, where the kings actually lived. I am of the opinion that Tazaung-mon is celebrated as a Festival of Lights in Lower Burma simply because the regular Festival of Lights one month earlier is usually rained out. Unlike that in Upper Burma, the monsoon here remains strong at the Full Moon of Thadingyut. I may mention that in Lower Burma, Tazaung-mon is also celebrated with rowdyism and 'thieving'.

[1] Meru in Pali.

7

The Thirty-seven Lords

The list

In the previous chapter I explained how Anawrahta was
constrained to give some royal recognition to the existing cult
of the Thirty-six Lords with the Lord of the Great Mountain
as the chief *Nat*, and how Anawrahta added the guardian-
god of Buddhism, whose name was Sakra in Pali and Thagya
in Burmese, to the list, thus making it the cult of 'Thirty-
seven Lords' instead of 'Thirty-six Lords'. In addition, he set
up their images on the platform of the Shwezigone pagoda
that he built. The list had closed at thirty-six before Anawrahta, and it needed Anawrahta's prestige and power to
change the number from thirty-six to thirty-seven. After
Anawrahta no one dared to assume authority to change the
number. However, with the passing of time the list varied,
for some old *Nats* were displaced by new *Nats*, and the personalities of later characters became merged with those of
earlier ones. This has misled some European scholars into
scoffing at the number thirty-seven and to proceed to point
out the existence of the 'thirty-eighth', 'thirty-ninth' and
'fortieth' *Nats*. In actual fact, the number of *Nats* worshipped
in Burma amounts to well over a hundred, but the *Nats*
associated with the cult of the Thirty-seven Lords number
at one time no more and no less than thirty-seven. From
time to time official lists of the thirty-seven *Nats* were drawn
up by royal authority, and under King Bodawpaya such a
list was compiled by the Minister Myawaddi. Because of the

historical accident of the fall of the Burmese kingdom in 1885, Myawaddi's list became the final official list.[1]

The list recognized by the hereditary attendants at Shwe-zigone also became fixed and finalized only by the time of the fall of the kingdom of Pagan. That it had varied from time to time even during the Pagan period can be seen from the fact that some of the *Nats* mentioned in the list appeared after Anawrahta had set up the images of the *Nats* on the platform of the Pagoda. The images are crude and primitive, and they were gathered from the various *Nat*-shrines in various parts of the country and set up at the Pagoda. The King's architects and sculptors, whose handiwork still adorns the Pagoda, were never allowed to touch them. Thus the images have stood throughout the centuries fixed and unchanged, although some of their identities and some of their names have changed from time to time. Thus, for example, Lord Sithu, who was unborn at the time the images were first set up, is now taken as represented by one of the images and he therefore has re-placed an older Sithu.

The Thirty-four Lords

I have already given in the chapter on the Lord of the Great Mountain an account of the King of the Gods, the Lord of the Great Mountain, and Lady Golden Face. I shall now give an account of the remaining Thirty-four Lords. By way of introduction, I may say that all of them were originally quite ordinary human beings, whose strange and sudden deaths, however, roused feelings of terror and pity in the minds of their contemporaries.

The Lady Golden Sides

The Lady Golden Sides, Lady Three Times Beautiful, the Little Lady with the Flute, the Brown Lord of Due South, and the White Lord of the North are Pyu gods who were

[1] For Myawaddi's list see Appendix 1 to this chapter.

worshipped at Prome and were later worshipped at Pagan. The Lady Golden Sides obtained her name from the special robe she was entitled to wear, a robe with trimmings of gold. She was from Mindon, a town behind Thayetmyo on the right bank of the Irrawaddy. According to legend, she was either the *Naga*-King's daughter, who was forsaken by her human husband, or a human woman who was forsaken by her *Naga* lover, as a result of which she died of grief.

My family has belonged to Mindon since the Prome period of Burmese history and, until the First Anglo-Burmese War of 1824, Mindon was the capital of the 'Seven Hill Districts' which lay between Arakan and the Irrawaddy. The Lady Golden Sides was one of my family ancestors and, according to tradition in our family, she was appointed to succeed her husband as the king's representative at Mindon, as both her sons were in the service of the king at Prome. (It may be mentioned that under the Burmese kings no office was hereditary but, other things being equal, the son or brother, or occasionally the widow of a deceased official, was often chosen by the king as his successor.)

After her death Lady Golden Sides was worshipped as a *Nat*-goddess by the people of Mindon. When Prome fell some time later, the king and his people escaped across the Irrawaddy and remained as wandering refugees for some twelve years, spending three years at Mindon.[1] When the king and his followers migrated north to the region which was to become the kingdom of Pagan, they had added Lady Golden Sides to their list of Pyu gods and goddesses. Lady Golden Sides is still worshipped at Mindon, but she is worshipped in her own right as the guardian-goddess of the town, and not as one of the Thirty-seven Lords. It may be mentioned that in our family she is remembered but never worshipped, and according to our family tradition she died of grief when her two sons were executed by the king. Neither the local

[1] Tin & Luce, op. cit., p. 28.

tradition at Mindon nor our family tradition makes her a *Naga*. Yet the very old ritual song relating to her as one of the Thirty-seven begins with the words:

> For the golden *Naga* to wear,
> Bring we a robe of satin-velvet.

The song seems appropriate as it gives the emphasis to the robe of satin-velvet—the robe trimmed with gold, but it is difficult to understand how the goddess became associated with the cult of *Naga* worship. Her image at the Shwezigone Pagoda shows no trace of her connexion with the *Naga*. It is true that later figures found in various *Nat*-shrines all over the country show the goddess wearing a head-dress with the *Naga* hood, but the Goddess Golden Face is also shown in later wooden figures wearing the same type of head-dress and she has never been associated with the *Naga* in any way.

It may be that the Lady Golden Sides became merged with a *Naga*-goddess, for the worship of the *Naga*-dragon was prevalent in Tagaung on the upper Irrawaddy and traces of the cult of the *Naga*[1] still exist at Tagaung to the present day in the worship of 'Bobo Gyi of Tagaung', 'the Great Grandfather of Tagaung'. The cult spread to Pagan, and the Chronicles mention a king of Pagan, before Anawrahta, setting up a great image of the *Naga* in his garden for worship.[2] Before Pagan, the *Naga* is mentioned as one of the builders of the city of Prome. His tail was held by the King of the Gods while he moved around in a circle, thus marking the circumference of the city. Before the advent of Buddhism an image of the *Naga* was set up with those of the village gods and goddesses outside the eastern gate of a village. The mud volcanoes of Minbu still have a tradition that *Nagas* live beneath, and there still exist many villages whose names

---

[1] For the sake of completeness, some details of the cult of the *Naga* are given here. Further details will be found in the Appendix to this chapter.
[2] Tin & Luce, op. cit., p. 59.

refer to *Nagas*, as, for example, 'the *Naga*-Hole', 'the Male *Naga*', 'When the *Naga* Descends (into the earth)', 'When the *Naga* is Angry'. In the Popa Hills, and in some parts of the Shan States, there still remain traces of a snake-cult. It may well be that there was a *Naga* god or goddess among the Thirty-six gods, or even that the Tagaung Dragon was one of the Thirty-six, whom Anawrahta replaced with the *Nat*-spirit of one of his own heroes.

The Lady Three Times Beautiful

The second Pyu Goddess, the Lady Three Times Beautiful, was a village maiden whose beauty surpassed man's imagination. She was beautiful 'in the morning, at midday, and at night', and her fame reached the ears of her king, the great Duttabaung. He sent a nobleman to fetch her to be crowned queen of Prome. But like Kyansittha and the Peguan princess of Pagan, the nobleman and Three Times Beautiful fell in love on the way. When they reached the gates of Prome the nobleman went in alone and announced to the King, 'Great King, her face is beautiful, but her body is so monstrously fat that she cannot enter the gates of the city.' Duttabaung believed him and ordered that she be abandoned. A hut was built for her outside the city gates and she dwelt there, forgotten by the king and forsaken by her lover. She earned her living as a weaver. In course of time she gave birth to a little girl and then died of grief and became a *Nat*.

The Little Lady

Her daughter is the third Pyu Goddess, the Little Lady, and her name originally meant 'the Little Lady with the Flute'. However, the image at Pagan and later wooden images do not show her playing a flute. As Hindu gods, especially Krishna, a reincarnation of Vishnu, are often shown playing on a flute, it seems logical to assume that the Little Lady of Prome became merged with an earlier Hindu goddess. Among the Thirty-seven *Nats* the Little Lady is most charming, and she is the guardian-goddess of little children and school-boys and schoolgirls. When a Burmese child smiles in his sleep it is believed that the Little Lady is playing with him, and boys and girls on the eve of their annual school examinations make offerings of toys and tiny jackets and skirts to the little goddess. Whereas Golden Face, Golden Sides, and Three Times Beautiful are shown in the later wooden figures in the conventional attitude depicting grief, right hand on the left breast, the Little Lady is depicted as a plump little child, with her chubby hands hanging free in the conventional attitude of joy, and with long necklaces and large bracelets of solid gold.

The Lord of Due South and the Lord of the North

The Lord of Due South and the Lord of the North were brothers who held high office under King Duttabaung at Prome. They were tax officials, and the kingdom was divided into two main tax regions, the north and the south. The term 'due south' is used to distinguish this god from the Lord of the Great Mountain, as the Burmese words for 'south' and 'mountain' are the same. They are also known as the 'Brown Lord' and the 'White Lord' from the colour of the official robes they wore. They became so powerful and popular with the people that the king thought that they might rebel. According to the Chronicles[1] they were put to death by the king, but according to the tradition of the *Nat*-worshippers they lost their lives through the guile of the king. They were great pugilists, and the king made them box and wrestle with each other until both died through exhaustion. An old tradition makes them the sons of the Lady Golden Sides, but neither the local tradition at Mindon nor our own family tradition remembers them. The Lady Golden Sides did have two sons

---

[1] Tin & Luce, op. cit., p. 18.

serving the king at Prome. They were later executed, but no details of these sons are remembered.

Just as the Lady Golden Sides is worshipped by herself at Mindon, and not as a member of the pantheon of the Thirty-seven, the Lords Brown and White were worshipped separately from the others at Prome until recent years. In addition to their usual names, in the Prome area they were called 'the Lords of the Royal Cave', probably because their images were placed in a cave for worship. These two gods are unique among the Thirty-seven, because whereas the other gods are shown with the usual physical features of human beings, they are always shown with six hands each. Two of the hands are folded in an attitude of worship, and the other four hands are shown holding various weapons of war. They are dressed in the ancient uniform of Burmese army commanders, with war helmets on their heads. Obviously the *Nat* spirits of the Lords Brown and White had merged with some six-handed Hindu gods who were known to the Pyus at Prome. The worship of these five Pyu gods and goddesses was already in existence when the cult of the Lord of the Great Mountain came into being, but there were attempts made to link these five with the Lord of the Great Mountain and his sister, Golden Face. Some spirit-worshippers insisted that the Lady Golden Sides became the lover of Master Handsome while he was a fugitive at Mindon from Tagaung and, therefore, the Lords Brown and White were the sons of the Lady Golden Sides and Master Handsome. Moreover, in the Popa region the younger sister of Master Handsome and Golden Face, known as Youngest-Beautiful, has always been worshipped along with the Brother and Sister, although she has never been admitted to the circle of the Thirty-seven. Accordingly, some spirit-worshippers merged Three Times Beautiful with Youngest-Beautiful, which would also bring her daughter, the Little Lady, into the family of the Lord of the Great Mountain.

The Lord with the White Umbrella

The Lord with the White Umbrella, his Mother, and the Sole Lord of Preimma were the father, grandmother and step-brother of Anawrahta himself. In A.D. 906[1] a usurper seized the throne of Pagan after killing the king, one of whose queens fled the palace with the dead king's child in her womb. She stayed in hiding in a small village and gave birth to Kunhsaw. While the child was growing up the usurper had died and the throne passed to his son. The usurper's son himself was killed by Nyaung-u Sawrahan. Later, Kunhsaw became king of Pagan by popular acclaim and Nyaung-u Sawrahan was killed, leaving three queens, two of whom were already with child. Kunhsaw raised all three to be his queens, and the dead king's sons, Kyizo and Sokkate, were born. The third queen later gave birth to Kunhsaw's own son, Anawrahta. Kunhsaw treated Kyizo and Sokkate as if they were his own sons, and Kyizo was given the title of 'Sole Lord' with the village of Preimma as his fief. However, the two brothers, when they came of age, plotted together and deposed Kunhsaw by forcing him to become a monk. The new king, Kyizo, was accidentally killed near Popa Hill during a deer-hunt by a hunter who was shooting at a deer. Sokkate then became king, and Anawrahta had to wait some twenty-five years before he could rebel. He killed Sokkate in single combat and then offered the throne to his father, now an aged monk. On his father refusing, Anawrahta became king in A.D. 1044.

Kunhsaw's mother is shown in later wooden images in the conventional attitude of grief, but there is no tradition of her dying of grief, as in the case of Golden Sides and Three Times Beautiful. But she did see her husband, the king, dethroned and killed, and she lived in want and anxiety for years. Kunhsaw is worshipped as the Lord with the White Umbrella, but as Monk, not King, Kunhsaw. His images show him

[1] This date (given in the Chronicles) is obviously wrong, since Kunhsaw would be 138 years old in A.D. 1044.

wearing a monk's yellow robes. A king on becoming a monk would lose the insignia of kingship, but Anawrahta, on becoming king, 'arrayed his father in all the articles of pomp and use, and the five symbols of royalty,[1] and the White Umbrella was the most important of these symbols of royalty. Kyizo is worshipped not as king but as the popular young lord of the village of Preimma, but his images show him wearing the full regalia of a king. It should be noted that when Anawrahta came to the throne his royal father was still living, but by the time Buddhism was made the official religion of the country he was dead and being worshipped as a god.

The Elder and Younger Inferior Gold

The Elder Inferior Gold and the Younger Inferior Gold, the Royal Grandfather of Mandalay, the Lady Bandy-Legs and the Old Man by the Solitary Banyan Tree were contemporaries of Anawrahta himself, and to this list I would also add the Lady Hunch-Back. The Elder and Younger Inferior Gold were famous sons of a famous father, Byat-ta.[2] Byat-ta was executed and his widow died of a broken heart and, stricken with remorse, Anawrahta sent for the two children, and gave them presents of gold. To be given presents of gold by the king was a mark of special favour for a child, but as presents of pure gold could be given only to princes of royal blood, the gold given to the two young boys was deliberately made a little impure. Elder and Younger Inferior Gold were placed under a tutor (who was also a minister) at Mandalay, and when they were fifteen years of age they joined the army. They gained great distinction in Anawrahta's 'Chinese Campaign',[3] but when the army returned they were executed at the village of Taung-byon near Mandalay for a minor breach of discipline. Anawrahta had to be a stern disciplinarian, and he had to be ruthless whenever there was a possibility of a

[1] Tin & Luce, op. cit., p. 64.　　[2] See Ch. 6.　　[3] Tin. & Luce, op. cit., p. 81.

91

rebellion or mutiny. In the case of the two brothers, their disobedience was considered specially dangerous because the cult of the superman could have been revived round the two brothers. They were the sons of a 'mighty man of endeavour' and a 'flower-eating ogress', and their exploits during the campaign had spread rumours of their supernatural powers.

However, the execution of the young heroes must have caused great dissatisfaction among the people. As a result, Anawrahta was constrained to declare that they had become gods and to appoint them 'the Lords of Taung-byon'. Just as the Popa Village was given as fief to the Lord of the Great Mountain, the village of Taung-byon was given as a fief to the two brothers. Their tutor was also executed and he died with great dignity, protesting that his guilt did not amount even to a 'finger-joint'. His images show him in the robes of a minister of state, with his right hand stretched out with the thumb placed on the top joint of the forefinger. This gesture and the phrase 'not as big as even a finger-joint' go together, and are used even at the present day in ordinary conversation. The ogress-mother who had died of grief has been worshipped at Taung-byon and at Popa since Anawrahta's days, but she is not included among the Thirty-seven.

The Ladies Bandy-Legs and Hunch-Back

The tutor's sister, Lady Bandy-Legs, was executed along with him. Lady Hunch-Back is grouped among the Ava gods and goddesses because the Lady Hunch-Back of the Ava period merged with the Lady Hunch-Back of the Pagan period. This can be known, firstly from the fact that she is listed among the Thirty-seven by the Attendants at the Shwezigone Pagoda; and secondly, from the ritual song connected with the royal tutor:

> I am the brother of two sisters,
> The Ladies Bandy-Legs and Hunch-Back.

The Old Lord of the Solitary Banyan Tree

The Old Lord of the Solitary Banyan Tree was one of the Mon princes who were taken captive to Pagan from the city of Thaton, together with their king, and he later died of leprosy. Again, this god obviously merged with an older god associated with the worship of the banyan tree. The Burmese believed in tree gods and worshipped large trees as the abode of these gods even before the coming of Buddhism. The banyan tree was worshipped, and water was poured on it as an offering in the parched months of summer. With the coming of Buddhism this ceremony of offering water to the banyan tree became a Buddhist ceremony, because the banyan tree is closely associated with the Buddha. Perhaps the Lord of the Banyan Tree, Lady Bandy-Legs and Lady Hunch-Back merged with earlier gods associated with some deformity of body. Just as some primitive peoples considered deformed persons evil and sinister, so others considered them to be occult and sacred.

Lord Sithu

Lord Sithu, the Young Lord of the Swing, the Valiant Lord Kyawswa, Captain of the Main Army Aung-Swa, the Royal Cadet and the Lady Golden Words may be grouped together as they lived in the later Pagan period. Lord Sithu was the great king Alaungsithu (A.D. 1112–1167), who followed his grandfather Kyansittha on the throne. As he lay sick and dying in extreme old age he was killed by his son, Narathu (A.D. 1167–1170). His name was merged with that of an earlier Sithu, who was a son of an early king of Pagan, Theinsun (A.D. 734–744). This earlier Sithu and his brother Kyawswa were the sons of the northern queen, and they were suspected of plotting to do away with the heir to the throne, the son of the senior or southern queen. Accordingly, they were

93

exiled, and they wandered all over the country having various adventures until they settled down at Myaung-tu village and started to dig irrigation canals. But the two brothers began to suspect each other of treachery, and in a fight with bare hands each killed the other. Thus, the image of Lord Sithu, when Anawrahta set it up, represented the earlier Sithu, but the greater personality of King Alaungsithu later obliterated the personality of his namesake.

The Young Lord of the Swing was the grandson of Alaungsithu. His father was the crown prince Minshinsaw, who became king after Alaungsithu's assassination, but only for a day, as he was poisoned by his brother, the murderer of Alaungsithu. The Young Lord of the Swing, after the usual initiation ceremony of a Burmese boy, was spending some time at a monastery as a novice, but while playing on a swing in the monastery grounds, he fell and was killed instantaneously.

The Valiant Lord Kyawswa

The Valiant Lord Kyawswa was originally the brother of the earlier Sithu and the image at the Shwezigone Pagoda represented this Kyawswa, but his personality has been merged with three later Kyawswas. One of the ministers of Alaungsithu had four sons, all in the king's service, but whereas the elder three were serious and well-behaved, the youngest Kyawswa was a wild young man who married the daughter of the manufacturer of toddy-wine from Popa village, for the girl was so beautiful and the father so skilful as a maker of toddy. He spent his time in cock-fighting, setting off fireworks and drinking, and he finally died of drink. This was the second Kyawswa. The last king of Pagan, Narathihapate (1254–1287), had three sons, Uzana, Governor of Bassein, Thihathu, Governor of Prome, and Kyawswa, Governor of Dalla. After the fall of Pagan to the Tartars, Thihathu forced the king, his father, who had come to Prome, to swallow poison on threat of death by the sword. He then went to Bassein, found Uzana ill in bed, and promptly hacked him to death. Thihathu then turned his attention to Kyawswa, but he accidentally shot himself with an arrow as he was setting his cross-bow, and Kyawswa returned to Pagan as the surviving heir. But soon he was strangled to death by some of his governors who wanted to seize the throne. This was the third Kyawswa. After the fall of Pagan the kingdom broke up into various petty kingdoms, until two new kingdoms emerged, namely Ava in Upper Burma and Pegu in Lower Burma. Minhkaung (1401–1422) of Ava and Razadarit (1385–1423) of Pegu then struggled for supremacy. Minhkaung's son, Minye Kyawswa, born in 1391, was a brilliant soldier, and he took part in a campaign at the early age of thirteen. He led the life of a professional soldier and was a hard drinker. He became the commander-in-chief of the Burmese army in 1409 and won a series of brilliant victories, but in 1417 he was taken prisoner after being severely wounded and died shouting defiance with his last breath. This was the fourth Kyawswa.

However, it is the personality of the second Kyawswa which has dominated the personalities of the others, as the following extract from the ritual song connected with the Valiant Lord Kyawswa will show:

Do you not know me? Have you not seen me at cock-fights? Have you not seen me letting off fireworks? Many times have I fallen prostrate in the gutter, drunken with my wife's wine, and many times have I been picked up by the loving hands of pretty village maidens.

Do you not know me, the god with the wine bottle, the famous Lord Kyawswa? If you do not like me, avoid me. I admit I am a drunkard. My neighbours despise me, but do I care for public opinion? If they do not like me, they can avoid me.

It is not surprising that Lord Kyawswa is considered the guardian-god of rogues and vagabonds.

Captain of the Main Army Aungswa

Captain Aungswa was in the First Army of the Kingdom, whose commander-in-chief was the Crown Prince who later became King Narapatisithu (1173–1200). His elder brother, King Naratheinhka (1170–1173), fell in love with Narapatisithu's wife, and sent him and his army to the frontier after falsely announcing that a rebellion had broken out there. The Crown Prince had to go, but he had a suspicion that there was something wrong, and left his own horse and his trusted officer Nga Aung Pyi at Pagan to wait and watch. After a few days the King seized the Crown Princess and made her his fourth queen. Nga Aung Pyi rode post-haste in the wake of the army, but when he reached a river he mistook a sandbank glittering in the moonlight for water and thought the river too wide to cross safely at night. So he slept whilst waiting for daylight to appear. The Crown Prince was only a little distance away on the other side of the river, and he became full of forebodings as he heard the neighing of his horse. When morning dawned Nga Aung Pyi swiftly crossed the river, caught up with the army, and broke the news to the Crown Prince, who was at first grateful to his officer but later asked, 'Where did you sleep last night?' 'On the other side of the river,' was the reply. The Crown Prince regretted the unnecessary delay, and in his anger executed Nga Aung Pyi for neglect of duty. But as the dead body floated downstream he was full of remorse and ordered that the spirit of Nga Aung Pyi be worshipped as one of the Thirty-seven, thus replacing an earlier god. But although Master Aung Pyi is included in the list maintained by the Attendants at Shwezigone Pagoda, he is dropped in the later lists.

The Crown Prince then selected his best Captain, Aungswa, and ordered him to lead an advance party to Pagan. 'I will give you one of his queens if you can kill the King,' promised the Crown Prince. So, as the army turned back and marched towards Pagan, Captain Aungswa and his men went ahead, raided the palace and killed the King. When the Crown Prince arrived on the scene and was on the point of asking his gallant captain to make his choice among the three queens, the women wept and pleaded, 'We are your cousins, we are queens. Surely you would not give one of us to an ordinary army captain?' The King relented and said to Aungswa, 'I did make you the promise to give you a queen, but would you not be satisfied with the daughter of a minister?' The Captain said 'Pish!' in contempt. For this act of insubordination, which angered the King, Aungswa was executed. Later, in view of his past services, Aungswa was raised to the status of a god and added to the list of Thirty-seven, thus replacing an earlier god.

The Royal Cadet and Lady Golden Words

The Royal Cadet was the son of Sawmun-hnit, who was the son of Kyawswa, and who was put on the throne of Pagan by the usurpers after they had killed Kyawswa. But by that time Pagan had become a mere province, and so Sawmun-hnit was not really the king but the governor of Pagan, although because he was a direct descendant of the dynasty of Anawrahta he was given the regalia and the rank of a king. The young cadet spent his time cock-fighting instead of marching with the army. So he was put in stocks by the order of his father, but the punishment was too heavy for the frail lad and he died. His mother, the queen Lady Golden Words, died of grief on learning that her son had died in these tragic circumstances. Of these later Pagan gods, the non-inclusion of the Royal Cadet and his Mother in the list maintained by the Attendants at the Shwezigone Pagoda can be explained by the fact that the kingdom of Pagan ended with the death of Kyawswa, and Sawmun-hnit, as has been stated above, was a king merely in name, and the Chronicles correctly consider Kyawswa to be the last king of Pagan. With regard to the non-inclusion of the Little Lord of the Swing, it seems that Master

Aung Pyi replaced him, but this substitution was probably not accepted generally. Nga Aung Pyi is worshipped at the present day only in the region where he was executed. He is worshipped on his own, moreover, and not as one of the Thirty-seven Lords.

The remaining Eleven Lords

Of the remaining Eleven Lords, who are included only in the Shwezigone Attendants' list, the Lord of the White Elephant must have been a king. The Lord of the White Horse must have been an official or a soldier; sometimes he is merged with others, and thus the Royal Cadet and Master Aung Pyi are often identified as the Lord of the White Horse. In any case, the Lord of the White Horse has always been associated with the Burmese army. In the dark days of 1824 when the Burmese army was retreating before the British, regiments often stood firm and fought rear-guard actions, as men said the god on his white horse had been seen fighting against the enemy.

Pagan started as a cluster of nineteen villages, and the Lord of the Four Islands (i.e. island-villages in the Irrawaddy), the Lord of the Five Villages, and the Lord of the Ten Villages were all king's deputies who built up the new kingdom. The Lord of the Nine Towns is the guardian god of the irrigated region around Kyaukse, known as the 'Nine Districts'[1] and he is worshipped in the region even at the present day on his own, and not as one of the Thirty-seven. The Great Physician was probably a king's physician and the Lord of the Ninety-nine Shan States must have been the king's minister for the Shan States who had their own chieftains, or the chief of all the Shan Chieftains. The waters of the country were divided into three kinds by the Burmese, 'Tame Waters' or inland waters, 'Salt Waters' or the Deltaic or tidal waters, and 'Open Waters' or the waters of the open sea. Probably, the

---

[1] See Chapter 2.

Lords of the Salt Waters and the Open Ocean, and the Lady of the Tame Waters were officials of the king controlling navigation in the various kinds of 'Waters'. The Lady of the Tame Waters is still worshipped on her own in the districts in the vicinity of the Chindwin River, the large tributary of the Irrawaddy. The Lord of the Salt Waters, with the title of the 'Foremost Great Lord', became so popular in the Deltaic Region that around him a separate cult arose, and thus at the present day in Lower Burma the cult of the 'Foremost Great Lord' is more important than the cult of the Thirty-seven. Anawrahta and Alaungsithu continued the tradition of the Pyu kings in making sea voyages to nearby lands, and merchants and monks of Pagan travelled to Bengal and Ceylon. So, during the period, the Lord of the Open Sea was of great importance, but after the fall of Pagan the tradition of sea travel died out, and with it the worship of the Lord of the Open Sea.

The Lord of Five Elephants, the first in point of time among the gods of the post-Pagan period, was king of the new kingdom of Pinya which flourished from 1298 to 1364, when the capital shifted to Ava. He was the son of one of the three usurping brothers who murdered Kyawswa, the last king of Pagan. He reigned from 1343 to 1350, when he died of a sudden fever. Probably he replaced the Lord of the White Elephant of the Shwezigone Attendants' list. The Lord King, Master of Justice, was Tarabya, who was king of Ava in 1401 for seven months only. As he hunted in the forest he had an adventure with an alchemist and a goddess, lost his reason, and was assassinated by an attendant. Maung Po Tu was a merchant from the Pinya region; he was killed and eaten by a tiger at the foot of the Shan Plateau as he was returning from the Shan States with a cart-load of tea. This poor merchant stands alone in the august assembly of kings and officials who constitute the Thirty-seven. It seems that he has been placed in the post-Pagan period because he belonged to Pinya, which became a royal city only after the fall of Pagan. But in point of time he must have belonged to the Pagan period, and he must have come not from the royal city of Pinya, but from the small village which later became Pinya city, because his image riding astride a tiger is among the *Nat* images at the Shwezigone Pagoda. He is the guardian-god of traders and small merchants. The Queen of the Western Palace was the queen of Minhkaung the First, king of Ava from 1401 to 1422. As she played with her maids-of-honour in a cotton plantation she saw the apparition of the Valiant Lord Kyawswa, and she fainted and died. She merged with an earlier Queen of the Western Palace, probably the mother of Lord Sithu, who was originally included among the Thirty-seven at the Shwezigone Pagoda.

Aungpinle or 'the Sea of Victory' was an ancient natural lake near Ava which had served a reservoir for irrigation purposes since primitive times. The Lord of Aungpinle was an ancient god who was included in the original Thirty-seven. He was replaced by Ava Thihathu, the son of Minhkaung the First. Ava Thihathu became king in 1422. He neglected his erstwhile favourite queen and in 1426, at the queen's instigation, he was shot with an arrow and killed by one of his Shan Chiefs as he was superintending the construction of a canal at Aungpinle on elephant-back. As he was killed at Aungpinle while on an elephant he came to be known as 'Lord of Aungpinle, Master of the White Elephant'. Lady Bent, one of the concubines of the Lord of Aungpinle, died of grief, and she became merged with the Lady Bent who was one of the two sisters of the Royal Tutor executed along with the Brothers Inferior Gold.

Golden Nawratha was a grandson of Minhkaung the Second (1481–1502) and as he had plotted against the new king, his uncle Shwenankyawshin, he was executed by drowning in 1502. The Valiant Lord Aung Din was a son of King Anaukpetlun (1605–1628). He was very fond of opium and toddy-wine and died of an overdose of both. The Young Lord White was the son of an unidentified king of Ava, and he also died of an overdose of opium and wine. The Royal Novice was the son of an unidentified king of Ava and, like the earlier god the Young Lord of the Swing, he was spending a period of time in a monastery after the usual initiation ceremonies of a Burmese boy. The monastery was the Nget-pyit-taung Monastery (the monastery on the Bird-Shot Hill), which was famous throughout the Ava period. Here, the young novice died of snakebite while playing in the monastery compound.

Tabinshwehti (1531–1550) was one of the hero-kings of Burma, and he united Burma into one kingdom again, as in the days of Pagan. Coming to the throne of the small kingdom of Toungoo at the early age of fifteen, he soon showed his ability as commander and king. But success came too early for him and, without fresh fields to conquer, he took to drink, and was assassinated by one of his bodyguards at the age of thirty-four. The Lady from the North was the wife of Tabinshwehti's tutor, and as the time for the birth of her child approached she journeyed back to her village to be with her mother, but she gave birth to a child prematurely while on the way and died. She merged with an earlier Lady of the North belonging to the Pagan period. Her child survived and later became the Lord Minhkaung of Toungoo and was given the rank of king, although in actual fact he was the Governor of Toungoo, which had ceased to be the capital after Tabinshwehti made Pegu the capital of a united Burma. Lord Minhkaung was stricken with dysentery, and to restore his health he left the city for the countryside; but while travelling across an onion field he was overcome by the smell of onions and died suddenly. The King's Secretary was secretary to the Lord Minhkaung of Toungoo; according to one version he was sent by his lord to the forest to gather rare flowers and died of malaria; according to another version he was sent by his lord to pick some flowers from the palace-garden at night and was fatally bitten by a snake. He merged with an earlier King's Secretary of the Pagan period.

The King of Chiengmai was brought to Pegu as a prisoner of war by Bayinnaung (1551–1581), the great king who followed his brother-in-law Tabinshwehti on the throne. Although a prisoner, he was treated with consideration and courtesy, but he died of dysentery soon after. He was the last to be added to the pantheon of the Thirty-seven.

Analysis of the Thirty-six Lords

It has often been stated that the cult of the Thirty-seven Lords is merely a worship of dead heroes, but in actual fact, only a few of them are heroes. Of the hero kings, only Alaungsithu and Tabinshwehti are included, and Anawrahta himself and the great Kyansittha are not included. Of the eight 'mighty men of endeavour' who adorned the pages of Burmese history of the Pagan period, only two, the Brothers Inferior Gold, are worshipped. Moreover, ten women and three children are included. Leaving aside the King of the Gods, the remaining Thirty-six can be analysed according to the following tables:

9 kings, including the fallen king of Chiengmai, a prisoner of war at Pegu.

4 queens.

8 princes of the blood, including one from the fallen house of Thaton, a prisoner of war at Pagan.

11 in the service of the king, including four women, Golden Sides, an official in her own right, Lady Bandy-Legs, Lady Bent, and the Lady of the North, who belonged to families of officials in the service of the king.

4 commoners, the Lord of the Great Mountain, Three Times Beautiful, the Little Lady and Master Po Tu. The first three fell into the orbit of the great with dire consequences, but Master Po Tu was a real commoner.

Total   36

26 males, including (*a*) one monk, the Lord with the White Umbrella, and (*b*) two children, namely, the two novices.
10 women, including one child, the Little Lady.

Total   36

11 executed. If we exclude the later Lady Bent as belonging to the Ava period it will be   10

11 violent deaths. If we exclude the Second Valiant Lord Kyawswa as belonging to the Ava period it will be   .   .   .   10

DETAILS:

Murdered, 5 (it will be 6, if we include the First Kyawswa).
Died of wounds, 1 (the Fourth Kyawswa).
Suicide, 1 (the Lady Golden Face).
Snakebite, 2.
Eaten by tiger, 1.
Accidental, 1 (fell down from swing).

8 deaths brought about by 'sudden' illness or dreaded disease. If we include the Second Kyawswa as belonging to the Ava period it will be   9

103

DETAILS

Old Man of the Banyan Tree: leprosy.

The Lord of Five Elephants: sudden fever.

Queen of the Western Palace: death through fright.

Valiant Lord Aung Din and the Young Lord White: overdose of opium.

The Lady of the North: childbirth.

Minhkaung of Toungoo: smell of onions, and dysentery.

King of Chiengmai: dysentery.

The Second Kyawswa: overdose of wine.

4 died of grief. If we include the Lady Bent as belonging to the Ava period it will be   5

Total 34   34

2 Plus the Lord with the White Umbrella and the Royal Mother. The Royal Mother might have died of grief, but certainly not the Lord, who lived on to see his son Anawrahta restored to the throne   .   2

Total 36   Total 36

The tragic lives of the Thirty-six

It will be seen that out of the Thirty-six, thirty-five suffered tragic and violent deaths. Even the exception, the Lord with the White Umbrella, was a tragic figure—a king who regained his father's throne from the usurpers, only to lose it again; a king who ascended the throne amidst popular acclaim, only to be deposed with no hand lifted to defend him; a king who started his reign with such rich promise of achievement and glory, only to find that his hopes came to

naught, and who waited and waited for years after being
deposed for someone to come to his aid; we can glimpse a
broken heart behind these words to his son Anawrahta, 'I am
old to look upon, old in years. Be thou king thyself.'

The tragic lives of the Thirty-seven and the manner in
which they died roused feelings of horror and pity in the
minds of the people. It was a gesture of defiance against Fate
and Death on the part of the common people that they were
worshipped as gods and goddesses after their death. It was
not terror of their supernatural power that caused the people
to worship them, for who could be afraid of the Little Lord
of the Swing, or of the Little Novice, who in his helplessness
and inexperience was killed by a snake, or of the Little Lady
with the Flute whose melodies cheered a sleeping babe? For
that matter, who could be afraid of the Royal Tutor, who
died protesting his innocence, of the Ladies Bent and Bandy-
Legs, of the poor prisoner, the Leper Prince? Or, of the Lady
with the Gold Trimmings on her robes of velvet, who ruled
over Mindon villages with such grace and kindness, of the
poor Drunken Lord, whom his fellows despised but the village
maidens loved, of poor Master Po Tu with his cartload of tea?

Their overlordship

The term Thirty-seven *Nats* is never used by their devotees; the proper term is 'Thirty-seven Lords', and Lords they
were. The Lord of the Great Mountain gained Popa village as
his fief from King Thinlikyaung, the Brothers Inferior Gold
obtained the village of Taung-byon as their fief from Anawrahta, Captain Aung Pyi obtained a village near the scene of
his death as his fief from Narapitisithu. These were royal
lords, but all the others were lords by popular consent. It was
for protection that the people made their offerings to them,
and they never interfered with the lives of those who were not
their devotees. Their overlordship was both territorial and
personal. In the vicinity of their shrines all must show their

respect. But outside the territorial limits of their shrines they would demand respect only from their devotees and would afford protection and favour in return. At the present day the idea of overlordship has disappeared, for when the Burmese king fell in 1885, all his lords, including the Thirty-seven, fell with him. However, the devotees of the cult still turn to them for protection and assistance.

They are anthropomorphic

The cult of the Thirty-seven Lords is anthropomorphic, and offerings of food, pickled tea, toddy-wine, and clothes are made, and some gods have special likes and dislikes. Thus the Old Man by the Banyan Tree dislikes meat and drink, the Brothers Inferior Gold, being the sons of a Muslim, do not like pork. The Lord of the Mountain dislikes offerings of *Saga* flowers, for he was tied to a *Saga* tree when he was burnt to death, and the Lord Minhkaung of Toungoo dislikes food flavoured with onions, for did he not die of a strong smell of onions? In other words, to their devotees the Lords are real persons.

This anthropomorphic cult has affected Burmese Buddhism, for since the days of Pagan up to the present day offerings of food and even robes are made to the images of the Buddha both in private houses and at the pagodas. In times of national danger and disaster the people believe that the Thirty-seven Lords are always with them. Men said that when the Tartar army invaded the country the Lords fought side by side with the soldiers, and some of them were wounded by the Tartar arrows; that the Lord of the White Horse and the Brothers Inferior Gold shared the sorrow and the shame and the glory of the Burmese soldier retreating from the British; that the gilded images of the Thirty-seven Lords at the king's palace shed human tears when Theebaw, the last king of Burma, was taken away a prisoner in the hands of the British army; and that when great fires broke out in the golden city of Mandalay after a Japanese air-raid in April 1942, the Brothers Inferior Gold were seen fighting the fires shoulder to shoulder with the stricken people. The great king Anawrahta might destroy their shrines and remove their images to his Shwezigone Pagoda, the great king Bayinnaung might issue edict after edict constraining their worship, but the gods and goddesses have remained ever enshrined in the hearts of their people.

APPENDIX 1

List of the Thirty-seven Lords

1. Thagyamin (the King of the Gods)
2. The Lord of the Great Mountain
3. Princess Golden Face
4. Lady Golden Sides
5. Lady Three Times Beautiful
6. The Little Lady with the Flute
7. The Brown Lord of Due South
8. The White Lord of the North
9. The Lord with the White Umbrella
10. The Royal Mother (of No. 9)
11. The Sole Lord of Pareim-ma
12. The Elder Inferior Gold
13. The Younger Inferior Gold
14. The Lord Grandfather of Mandalay
15. The Lady Bandy-Legs
16. The Old Man by the Solitary Banyan Tree
17. Lord Sithu
18. The Young Lord of the Swing
19. The Valiant Lord Kyawswa
20. Captain of the Main Army Aungswa
21. The Royal Cadet
22. His Mother, the Lady Golden Words

23. The Lord of Five Elephants
24. The Lord King, Master of Justice
25. Maung Po Tu
26. The Queen of the Western Palace
27. The Lord of Aungpinle, Master of White Elephants
28. The Lady Bent
29. Golden Nawrahta
30. The Valiant Lord Aung Din
31. The Young Lord White
32. The Lord Novice
33. Tabinshwehti
34. The Lady of the North
35. The Lord Minhkaung of Toungoo
36. The Royal Secretary
37. The King of Chiengmai

According to Minister Myawaddi and the devotees of the cult at the present day, the *Nats* numbered 1 to 22 belonged to the pre-Pagan and Pagan periods and the rest to the Ava and Toungoo periods of Burmese history. However, according to the list recognized by the hereditary attendants of the *Nat* images at the Shwezigone Pagoda, we find that (i) Nos. 1 to 17, 19, and 20 are included; (ii) Nos. 18, The Young Lord of the Swing, 21, The Royal Cadet and 22, The Lady Golden Words are not included; (iii) Nos. 23, The Lord of the Five Elephants, 25, Maung Po Tu, 26, The Queen of the Western Palace, 27, The Master of White Elephants from Aungpinle Lake, 34, The Lady of the North, and 36, The Royal Secretary are included as belonging to the Pagan period, for the attendants do not recognize any *Nat* who belonged to a later period than Pagan as one of their Thirty-seven, and (iv) the following twelve *Nats* complete the list of Thirty-seven:

1. Master Aung Pyi
2. The Lord of the White Elephant
3. The Lord of the White Horse

4. The Lord of the Nine Towns
5. The Lord of the Four Islands
6. The Lord of the Five Villages
7. The Lord of the Ten Villages
8. The Great Physician
9. The Lord of the Ninety-nine Shan States
10. The Lady of the Tame Waters (i.e. Inland Waters)
11. The Lord of the Salt Water Lands (i.e. the Irrawaddy Delta)
12. The Lord of the Open Ocean

APPENDIX 2

The Cult of the *Naga*

The Cult of the *Naga* was the one pre-Buddhist cult which did not recover from Anawrahta's suppression. At the present day the *Naga* is not worshipped at all, and there remain only two faint traces[1] of the original cult. As part of the initiation ceremony, the Burmese boy is 'shown' to the *Naga* at the western gate of an Upper Burmese village, and people avoid, as much as possible, going in a direction which is not 'according to the *Naga*'s head'. In the first, second and twelfth months of the Burmese year, the *Naga*'s head is turned towards the west, with the tail pointing east. In the sixth, seventh and eighth months this process is reversed. In the third, fourth and fifth months the head faces the north and the tail the south. This process is reversed in the ninth, tenth and eleventh months.

If one goes into the *Naga*'s mouth, disaster will result, and if one goes against the direction of the *Naga*'s scales, ill-luck will follow; for example, during the months in which the

[1] In addition to local traces at Tagaung, Popa and Shan States, as already mentioned above.

Naga's head is turned towards the east, one must absolutely avoid journeys from due east to due west, and avoid as much as possible journeys from due west to due east. The origin of the belief can no longer be traced and it is not possible to know, or even guess, which particular *Naga* is being referred to; in fact, if is not even known whether this *Naga* is in the sky or at the bottom of the ocean, or in the bowels of the earth.

As has been stated above, the worship of the *Naga* was prevalent in the kingdom of Tagaung. The Burmese *Naga* is similar in many ways to the Indian *Naga* and the Chinese Dragon, but it is difficult to say whether the worship of the *Naga* was originally a native cult or borrowed from the neighbouring regions of Manipur and Yunnan. Moreover, the worship of the *Naga* could have developed from the worship of the snake and, as has been noted above, in the Shan state and at Popa there are traces of a snake-cult. However, in these regions it is not so much the snakes, but their *Nat* masters who are worshipped. Thus, the Burmese snake-charmer goes to the Popa region, makes his offerings to the Popa *Nats*, promises to bring back the snakes within three years, and then proceeds to trap some cobras. The Burmese consider the *Naga* to be half animal and half spirit and do not identify it with the snake, with the result that, unlike the Southern Indians, they set upon and kill snakes, including cobras, whenever they find them.

The Burmese *Naga* is dangerous when angered, and its mere frown turns the human being into ashes. Even when not angry its breath can blind a human being as it is so hot. It can assume human form and, on the whole, it is a benevolent being. The Burmese believe that *Nagas* live at the bottom of deep rivers, seas and oceans and in the bowels of the earth. Although they can fly in the air they do not do so too often because they will become exposed to attacks from their eternal enemies, the *galon* (*garuda*) birds. Just as the great

Asoka of India had *Naga* retainers, an early king of Pagan was, according to the Chronicles, attended by an army of *Naga* youths. *Naga* workmen helped in the building of a palace at Tagaung and, when the palace was completed, the king of the *Nagas* himself assisted in the coronation ceremonies of the king. A *Naga* king assisted in the foundation of the city of Prome and gave his daughter as a second queen to the king, Duttabaung, together with a wondrous ocean-going boat covered with *Naga*'s scales. However, towards the end of his reign there was a quarrel between the *Nagas* and the king, and as he was travelling in the boat near the seaport of Bassein, the *Nagas* appeared from below a whirlpool and took back their boat, with the result that the king was drowned. The whirlpool still exists at the present day and it is called the 'whirlpool of *Naga-yit*', which means 'where the *Nagas* twist and turn'. One of the early kings of Pagan, the hero Pyusawhti, was the ward of a *Naga* king and queen who lived in a hole in a garden on the side of a hill, and who were worshipped with offerings of food and flowers by the people of the nearby villages. The king of Pagan, Nyaung-u Sawrahan, whom Anawrahta's father dethroned, built Buddhist temples, but he also set up the image of a *Naga* in a garden for worship.[1]

The Naga in Buddhism

The cult of the *Naga* did not reappear after the death of Anawrahta, because long before A.D. 1056 Buddhist literature had modified the pre-Buddhist conception of the *Naga*, and the *Nagas* were shown to be adherents of Buddhism and devout worshippers of the Buddha. The *Naga* tradition in Buddhism began with an episode in the life of the Buddha. After attaining Buddhahood, the Buddha spent seven weeks in continuous meditation in the vicinity of the Bodhi Tree, and the sixth of the seven weeks was spent on the shore of the

---

[1] The religion of this king is discussed in Chapter 9.

Mucalinda Lake, a few yards away from the Tree; there blew
a great storm, and the *Naga* king, who lived in a tree nearby,
sheltered the Buddha by winding his coils seven times round
the meditating Buddha's body and holding his hood over the
Buddha's head.[1] The depiction of the meditating Buddha
protected by the coils of the *Naga* king later became a popular
motif in Buddhist art and sculpture. The Buddha subdued
one fierce *Naga* near a hermitage, and later the Great *Naga*
who lived on Mount Mayyu. A *Naga* king was present when
the relics of the Buddha were being distributed after the
cremation of the body. In the Buddhist literature of Ceylon,
the *Naga* appeared often. The Buddha made a special visit to
the north of Ceylon to bring peace between the *Nagas* who
were fighting among themselves. When the Branch of the
Bodhi Tree was being brought to Ceylon by sea, the *Nagas*
wanted it for themselves, but still afforded protection to the
ship bringing the Branch. When 'the Great Temple' was
being built in Ceylon to enshrine some relics of the Buddha,
the *Nagas* contributed the relics in their possession. In the
face of such established Buddhist tradition the Burmese *Naga*
could no longer be worshipped separately from the Buddha.

Kyansittha attempted to bring the cult under his control
by announcing that when he was hiding from the wrath of
Anawrahta, he was sheltered by a *Naga* lad. He later named
the particular place where this incident took place. Modern
scholars have tried to give a rational explanation to this
episode in Kyansittha's life by explaining that it was not a
Naga but a cobra that Kyansittha was referring to, or that it
was a young attendant from a nearby temple devoted to *Naga*
worship that gave Kyansittha protection. However, such
explanations are unnecessary when we remember Kyansittha's
contention that he was a reincarnation of Vishnu and that
he was a fellow-worshipper, in a previous existence, with the
Lord of the Great Mountain. Just as he allowed the builders

---

[1] The *Naga*'s name was Mucalinda, hence the name of the lake.

of his palace to devote one whole day to ceremonies connected with the worship of the Lord of the Great Mountain and one whole day to those connected with Vishnu, so he permitted them to devote a whole day to ceremonies involving the worship of the *Nagas*. But although many of his courtiers themselves took part in the ceremonies held by the builders to propitiate the *Nagas* who had been disturbed when the foundations of the palace were laid, there was no popular revival of the *Naga* cult.

When Kyansittha later found that the people had accepted the new Buddhist conception of the *Naga*, he built a beautiful pagoda at the place where he was supposed to have been protected by the *Naga* lad, and named it 'the *Naga-yone*' meaning 'robed by the *Naga*', referring to the 'robing' of the Buddha by the Naga Mucalinda's coils. Later on, the name '*Naga-yone*' became a term to describe an image of the Buddha with the coils of the *Naga* round his body, or a pagoda with large *Naga* figures around it. In fact, up to the present day the *Naga* is the most popular motif in Burmese art, both religious and secular.

8

Initiation Ceremonies

The Shinbyu ceremony

Among present-day Burmese there exist two ceremonies
which can be described as initiation ceremonies, namely, the
Shinbyu ceremony and the 'Ear-boring' ceremony. The
Shinbyu ceremony marks the occasion of the entry of a
Burmese Buddhist boy into the Buddhist order of monks, and
the 'Ear-boring' ceremony marks the occasion of the boring
of a Burmese girl's ears so that she will be able to wear
jewelled earrings.

Every Burmese Buddhist boy has to enter the Buddhist
order of monks before he grows up to manhood. At the present
day, the age of the boy going through the *Shinbyu* ceremony
varies from about five to fifteen years. As part of the ceremony alms are offered to the monks, and friends are invited
to the reception given by the parents of the boy. It is an
occasion for gaiety and joy, but it is also a solemn occasion.
Solemn music, usually a royal march, is played. (In Burmese
music a royal march is slow and stately.) Then the boy's head
is shaved, and after a recital of formulae from the scriptures
the boy becomes a novice. So far as this part of the ceremony
is concerned it follows the Buddhist ceremony of initiation.

When a layman becomes a Buddhist monk, a ceremony
which has two parts is performed. The first part is the initiation, on the completion of which the layman becomes a
novice, and the second part is the ordination, on the completion of which the novice becomes a monk. The Burmese, therefore, have taken over the first part of the Buddhist ceremony
and grafted it on their own *Shinbyu* ceremony. The second

part of the ceremony is beyond the scope of the *Shinbyu* ceremony, as no person can be ordained as a Buddhist monk until he has attained the age of twenty years.

Pre-Buddhist elements in the ceremony

As in the case of all Burmese ceremonies and festivals, outwardly the *Shinbyu* ceremony is Buddhist; but it also contains pre-Buddhist elements. The boy has to remain indoors and under the careful watch of his elders at least seven days before the ceremony, because it is believed that evil spirits are jealous of his approaching glory and will attempt to cause some accident which would make him *hors de combat* for the ceremony. Then, on the morning of the ceremony, dressed in the full regalia of a prince or a king and shaded with gold umbrellas, the boy is put on a horse[1] and taken in procession round the town or village. As the procession gaily passes through the village, the young men of the village who attend on the boy during the procession and the ceremony will keep shouting, '*Shwe*', meaning '(to be) wet'. Often the leader will shout out, 'May the fields be . . .', and the other young men will act as the chorus and shout out, '*Shwe*'.

> 'May the fields be . . . '
> 'Wet.'
> 'May the streams be . . .'
> 'Wet.'
> 'May the breasts of the boy's mother be . . .'
> 'Wet.'
> 'May the breasts of the boy's sister be . . .'
> 'Wet.'

When the procession reaches the western gate of the village it stops for some minutes, during which time the boy has to sit upright on the horse and remain still, for he is being shown to the guardian-spirit of the village. Therefore, this part of

[1] Or an elephant if one is available.

the ceremony is known as 'the *Nat*-Showing Ceremony'. The boy then returns in procession to his parents' home. After he has been thus 'officially' returned to the parents, the young men will attempt to 'steal' the boy when the parents are not looking and, if successful, they will keep him hidden until the harassed parents 'redeem' him by paying a small fee.

Its social significance

Until the annexation of the country by the British in 1886 and the resulting changes in Burmese society, the *Shinbyu* ceremony had a deep social significance. The ceremony then was performed only when the boy had attained puberty and was fifteen or sixteen years of age. In those days the village monastery was also the village school, and thus the boy was no stranger to the monastery at the time of the ceremony. Since he was about six years old he had been attending the monastery, learning his lessons during the day, going round the village with the monks in the morning as they 'begged' for alms, and playing with the other boys of the monastery in the evenings. The initiation ceremony signified that his school days were over, and thus for him it was in some ways a graduation ceremony. The village maidens had never taken any notice of him until his *Shinbyu* ceremony, but now many a maiden waited hopefully his 'return from the monastery', as can be seen from the following folk-song:

> In front of this little maiden's house.
> There are one or two clumps of *sattha-phu*[1] flowers,
> The Parrots are pecking at them.
> Oh, Masters Golden Parrots, please spare the flowers,
> For they are meant to await the return from the monastery
>   of my beloved,
> When I shall adorn his ears with flowers.[2]

---

[1] *Satthaphu = Hsat-thwa-hpu = Pandanus tectorius.*
[2] A Burmese village maiden wore (and still wears) flowers in her hair, but the village youth wore them on his ears.

After the ceremony the boy remained as a novice for one or two months, or even longer, and then when he became a layman again, he was a fully-fledged young man. He would join the gay and merry throng of young bachelors of the village, and the village maidens would look askance at him. He would now be earning his own living, and his elders would encourage him to marry and set up a house. But to the young men of the village he was still a greenhorn, and he awaited with eagerness a second initiation. If the *Shinbyu* ceremony was a test of his intellect and moral character, the second initiation was a test of his courage and manliness.

The second initiation involved tattooing the young man. The Burmese had two kinds of tattoos, those for 'decoration' and those for 'magic', that is, for physical prowess and for invulnerability. The first tattoo for the young man was merely for 'decoration' and was a social necessity. The second, which would be for magical powers, would come later in life and by his own choice. Tattooing was a very painful process and the young man would bite his lips until blood flowed out, so that he should not cry out in pain; for should he utter a squeal or a shriek, it would be greeted with loud laughter on the part of his companions, and for days after he would be the butt of their jests.

Why is the boy dressed regally?

Why is the boy in the *Shinbyu* ceremony dressed as a king and why is he mounted on a horse? Before answering this question we have to note that whereas mounting a horse was a common thing for a Burmese boy in the days of the kings, being dressed as a prince or king was not only unusual but generally not permitted by law. Burmese society in many ways was a classless society in that there was a general absence of material inequalities, but the king insisted that the difference between himself and his officials, on the one hand, and the rest of his people, on the other, should be clearly marked. For that reason great emphasis was laid on marked differences in dress, and the king's regalia, and the robes and uniforms of his officials, were given great prominence. When the king appeared before the public he might not always come riding on a richly caparisoned elephant or horse, or borne on a golden litter; he might come walking, but he would be wearing the golden chains of majesty, the jewelled sword of power, and the golden shoes of royalty. He would be in the shade of the white umbrellas and the gold umbrellas which his attendants held over his head. To wear a dress in imitation of the king's regalia and the robes of his officials was treason, certain to be punished with instant death. But the boy in a *Shinbyu* ceremony, and actors in a play, were exempted from the operation of this law.

To return to the question, why is the boy dressed as a prince or king? The usual answer which will be given by the Burmese is that the boy is following the path of purity followed by Prince Siddhartha, who forsook his luxurious life of a prince to become a recluse and later the Buddha, and therefore the boy is, in effect, enacting the scene of Prince Siddhartha's renunciation of the world. But this explanation is merely an afterthought meant to give a Buddhistic basis to a pre-Buddhistic ceremony, just as Buddhistic explanations are given for many Burmese festivals which now seem to be Buddhistic, but which originated in pre-Buddhistic times.

The word *Shin* means 'monk', but it can also mean 'lord' or 'king'. Of course, from the way *Shin* is now spelt in Burmese, Burmese scholars will deny that it can mean 'king' and will say that it can mean only 'monk'. But the spelling itself is likely to be a later innovation, and colloquially *Shin* can have both these meanings. The phrase *Shinbyu* means 'to make a monk', but it can also mean 'to make a king'. The boy who is going to be initiated is called a *Shin-laung*, which means 'he who would be a monk', but it can also mean 'he who would be a king'.

In Burmese society, although the king and his officials were at the top of the social structure, everyone could hope to be king one day, and as the king's officers constituted a nobility by talent and not by birth, even the humblest peasant, if he had the ability, could hope to become an official of the highest rank. Burmese folk-lore is full of stories of poor boys becoming kings, and chronicles mention many instances of persons 'not of the royal bone' becoming kings. In early Burmese history, kings were elected by the free choice of the people, just as the village headman was elected by popular acclaim, and right up to the final fall of the Burmese kingdom in 1886 the theory was that the king ruled by choice of the people. Even after the establishment of the first Burmese empire under King Anawrahta, we find that the office of king could be filled by election; the great Kyansittha became king by popular acclaim, after the earlier royal line suddenly ended with the death of King Sawlu, Anawrahta's son. Therefore, when a Burmese boy entered manhood, he was qualified to be even the king of the country. Viewed against the background of these Burmese beliefs, the royal dress of the boy of the *Shinbyu* ceremony was originally meant to symbolize the fact that the boy was going to attain maturity and manhood.

The ceremony of 'showing to the *Nat*-spirits' had its origins in pre-Buddhist times. In many villages in Upper Burma until recently, the boy was shown not only to the *Nat* guardian but also to the *Naga* guardian of the village. Before Anawrahta's time the images of the *Nat* guardian and the *Naga* Dragon were placed in shrines at the eastern gate of the village and, as described above, after Anawrahta the worship of the *Naga* was abandoned and the worship of the *Nats* remained only as an adjunct to Buddhism. The image of the *Naga* was destroyed and that of the guardian *Nat* was removed to the western gate of the village when it was decided to build a pagoda and a monastery at the eastern gate. It was to these fallen and forgotten gods that the boy was originally meant to be 'shown'.

The word *Shwe*, which is shouted with so much gusto by the young men during the *Shinbyu* procession, was originally a Burmese imitation of the Sanskrit word *Sri*, so magically potent and auspicious to the Hindus. The Hindu astrologers who had been attendants at the court of the Burmese kings since the early centuries of the Christian Era had used this word on all ceremonial occasions, especially at the coronation of the king. The custom of using this word doubtless soon spread far beyond the palace gates, and it came to be used at the *Shinbyu* procession as an auspicious word, for it seemed fitting that the same magic word which was used at the coronation of a king should be used at the ceremony which marked the occasion of the boy's entry into manhood, which would qualify him to be even a king.

The ceremony was once a fertility ritual

However, the word *Shwe* means '(to be) wet', and in the parched country of Upper Burma, the home of the early Burmese kingdoms, wetness and fertility were synonymous. The *Shinbyu* ceremony was usually, if not always, performed in the Burmese month of Tabaung (February/March).[1] The harvest had been collected, the countryside was parched, and it was hoped that enough rain would fall some nine or ten weeks later when the new growing season was due to begin. Therefore, the word *Shwe* was a word of invocation and a prayer for rain, and as such it was a magic word to procure fertility. The repeated references to women's breasts during the course of the shouting seem to indicate that the *Shinbyu* ceremony was originally regarded also as a fertility ritual. In fact, the pre-Buddhist initiation ceremony which later became the *Shinbyu* ceremony was probably part of a harvest festival.

[1] Tabaung is still the usual month for initiation ceremonies.

The goddess Pon-ma-Kyi

Nowadays, some time after the harvest has been gathered and usually on the Full Moon Day of Tabaung, the eleventh month of the Burmese year, the women of every household spend the whole night in making white and red cakes. At the first streak of dawn they go to the back of the house and offer them to a *Nat* named Pon-ma-Kyi, who is described as a goddess with big breasts and a huge belly. According to one theory it means 'Great Lady in Hiding', and according to another it is a popular mispronunciation of the name 'Pobba-Kyai', meaning the 'Friday Star'. In my opinion, both explanations are correct. The primitive harvest festival later became associated with the fertility planet of astrology, namely the Friday planet, and the primitive goddess of fertility became merged with the new god of the Friday planet. After Anawrahta, the worship of both the primitive goddess and the Friday planet had to be practised in 'hiding'.

Regarding this goddess also, there exists a Buddhist explanation. As the Buddha was preaching to an assembly of monks and layman a woman rushed in carrying a newborn child, and in great fear and anxiety she placed it at the Buddha's feet. She explained that on previous occasions when she had given birth to a child a frightful-looking ogress came and ate up the child, and this time, also, the ogress appeared and so she had come running to the Buddha to save her child. The Buddha saw the ogress waiting outside, not daring to come near him. He soothed the woman and also gently asked the ogress to come near. Then he explained to them that in a previous existence the ogress was a doe, and every time she gave birth to an infant deer a tigress came and ate up the little animal. At last, the doe died praying for revenge and now she was the ogress and the tigress was the woman. The Buddha preached to them and the ogress, stricken with remorse, undertook never to eat flesh again, and seized with pity the woman took the ogress to her home

122

and gave her shelter and food. At first, the neighbours resented the presence of the ogress and abused her. But the ogress bore them no ill-will, and when the growing season approached, out of gratitude for her kindness, the ogress told the woman that rainfall was going to be scanty that year and advised her to grow her crops on low ground. That year, as the ogress had forecast, rainfall was scanty. The next year the ogress told the woman that rainfall was going to be heavy and advised her to grow her crops on high ground. Again as the ogress had said, the rainfall that year was heavy. As the woman always followed her advice regarding the crops, and as the forecasts of the ogress were always correct, the woman became prosperous. She told her neighbours about the wisdom of the ogress in foretelling rainfall, so that the neighbours also consulted the ogress and gave her presents of food, with the result that prosperity and tranquillity prevailed in the village.[1]

Other pre-Buddhist beliefs in the ceremony

Other pre-Buddhist beliefs are also to be found in the *Shinbyu* ceremony. The belief that evil spirits are liable to do bodily harm to the boy during the period of seven days before the ceremony by causing an accident, seems illogical from the Buddhist viewpoint. The boy is to enter the noble order of monks, and surely the seven-day period is a time of merit and virtue during which evil spirits should be powerless and subdued. It seems that the belief originally belonged to a more primitive initiation ceremony, before the advent of Buddhism.

The tattooing ceremony must also have been part of that more primitive initiation ceremony. The 'stealing' of the boy by the young men and the payment of a fee to redeem

---

[1] The full story is given in the *Dhammapada Commentary*. See Burlingame, *Buddhist Legends*, Part I (Harvard Oriental Series).

him will remind one of the payment of 'stone fee' and 'bed-chamber fee' in Burmese marriages; the 'stone fee' is payable by the parents of the bride to the young men of the village, who will throw stones at the house of the bride on the night following the marriage until the fee is paid. And the young women of the village will prevent the bridegroom from entering the bridal chamber, and even 'kidnap' the bride until a small fee is paid by the bridegroom. These customs are still followed, but their primitive origins and significance are no longer known.

The ear-boring ceremony

Since prehistoric times Burmese women have bored their ears. Burmese men, also, have sometimes bored their ears, but the practice was never widespread. The male members of the royal family usually had their ears bored, and for the king this was obligatory. In the villages, no ceremony seems to have marked the occasion of the ear-boring of either women or men, but at the king's court the ear-boring was always accomplished with ceremony. For the royal princesses this ceremony was compulsory, and no princess could marry until her ears had been ceremoniously bored. For the king the ceremony was obligatory, because the ear-boring ceremony was a necessary prelude to the ceremony of coronation. Royal custom was followed in the city where the ear-boring of the daughters of officials or of richer families was a ceremony.

These days ear-boring ceremonies are common in towns, but not in villages. Even in towns, the ceremony is by no means obligatory. Moreover, the ear-boring ceremony is a simple ceremony; guests are invited and fed, the ears of the young maidens for whom the ceremony is being performed are pierced with a gold needle, in the presence of the guests; some elders give a few words of greeting and advice to the maidens, and the ceremony is over. There is no religious significance attached to the ear-boring ceremony.

9

The Ari Monks and the Introduction of Buddhism

UNTIL the advent of Anawrahta there seem to have existed initiation ceremonies for young women also. But the nature and purpose of these initiation ceremonies will always be open to conjecture, because the Ari monks who, before Anawrahta, held sway over every facet of religious life of the Burmese people, ever remain the subject of controversy. Anawrahta and the Chronicles would make out that the Aris were heretics who had to be suppressed before Buddhism could shine again in all its glory. It cannot be denied that they did oppose Anawrahta and the purer form of Buddhism that he introduced, and that he had no other course left to him but to persecute them by putting to death the more rebellious leaders of their order and disrobing the others and forcing them to join his army.

Asoka's religious mission

According to the Chronicles, legends of various pagodas, and oral traditions, Buddhism reached Burma even during the lifetime of the Buddha, but did not make a lasting impression. Then the great Asoka sent a religious mission to the kingdom of Thaton, in the same way as he sent religious missions to Ceylon and other countries of south-east Asia. This tradition of Asoka's religious mission to Thaton was doubted at first by European scholars, G. E. Harvey, for example, but in the last one or two decades the tradition has come to be accepted as a historical fact, and nowadays only the most conservative among European scholars of Burmese history challenge this tradition. The Chronicles insist that the kingdom of Prome was a Buddhist kingdom, and archaeological evidence now makes it clear that Theravada Buddhism did flourish at Prome.

The Great Ari

According to the Chronicles the Buddhism that was reintroduced by Asoka's mission flourished not only at Thaton and Prome, but also in the new kingdom of Pagan until the reign of King Thaittaing (A.D. 516–523), when it started to decay. The reasons given by the Chronicles for this decay were, firstly, that there existed in the new kingdom no copy of the Buddhist scriptures and, secondly, that a sect of heretical Buddhist monks, known as the 'Great Ari', gradually won royal support. Taking advantage of the patronage given to them by the kings, they debased the religion, until the climax was reached in the reign of Nyaung-u Sawrahan (A.D. 931–964).

The following extracts contain the main indictments of the Great Ari:

(a) Now the King was great in glory and power. At his cucumber plantation he made a large and pleasant garden, and he wrought and kept a great image of *Naga*. He thought it good thus to make and worship the image of *Naga*, because *Naga* was nobler than men and his power greater. Moreover he consulted the heretical Ari monks regarding the *zigon* pagodas in the kingdoms of Yathepyi and Thaton, and he built five pagodas—Pahtogyi, Pahtonge, Pahtothamya, Thinlinpahto, Seittipahto. In them he set up what were neither spirit-images nor images of the Lord, and worshipped them with offerings of rice, curry, and fermented drinks, night and morning. He was also known as Nattawkyaung-taga-minchantha.[1]

(b) Now the kings in that country for many generations had been confirmed in false opinions following the doctrines of the

[1] Tin & Luce, op. cit., p. 59.

thirty Ari lords and their sixty thousand disciples who practised piety in Thamahti. It was the fashion of these Ari monks to reject the law preached by the Lord and to form each severally their own opinions. They wrote books after their own heart and beguiled others into the snare. According to the law they preached, a man might take the life of another and evade the course of *karma* if he recited the formula of deprecation; nay, he might even kill his mother and his father and evade the course of *karma* if he recited the formula of deprecation. Such false and lawless doctrine they preached as the true doctrine. Moreover, kings and ministers, great and small, rich men and common people, whenever they celebrated the marriage of their children, were constrained to send them to these teachers at nightfall, sending, as it was called, the flower of their virginity. Nor could they be married till they were set free early in the morning. If they were married without sending to the teacher the flower of their virginity, it is said that they were heavily punished by the king for breaking the custom.[1]

Nyaung-u Sawrahan

According to the Chronicles Nyaung-u Sawrahan was a cucumber planter before he became a king. His name means 'the Lord Monk of Nyaung-u', which is a village near Pagan. Like Popa Sawrahan before him, he must have been a monk before he became king, and must have been famous for his knowledge of magic and astrology. His other title mentioned in the extract means 'the Happy Royal Builder of *Nat* Shrines', and so he must have been a *Nat* worshipper, in addition to being a worshipper of the *Naga*. However, he was a devout Buddhist also, because he built, in addition to the pagodas mentioned in the extract, a Buddhist Ordination Hall, which act of merit was recorded in an inscription. In fact, he was the only king before Anawrahta to be mentioned in the inscriptions. Surely, the Aris that he worshipped could not have been so depraved if they needed and used a Buddhist Ordination Hall.

[1] Tin & Luce, op. cit., p. 70.

The offering of alms-food

The offering of alms-food to the Buddha images was a practice that prevailed both before and after Anawrahta, and is still an accepted religious practice. But it involves an anthropomorphic conception of the Buddha, which is more logical in Mahayana Buddhism than in Theravada Buddhism, and is also akin to the primitive practice of offering alms-food to the *Nats*. Rice-wine and toddy-wine were and are offered to *Nat* spirits, and perhaps that was why they were also offered to the Buddha images by Nyaung-u Sawrahan. It is difficult to understand what the Chronicles meant by the phrase 'what were neither spirit images nor images of the Lord', because the Burmese term *Nat* would have covered the gods of any religion.

The heresies of the Aris

According to the Chronicles the Aris were guilty of two great heresies: first, they insisted on interpreting the Buddhist scriptures in their own way, and, secondly, they held that any sin could be condoned by the recitation of a particular religious formula of prayer. Obviously the Chronicles were prejudiced against the Aris, and in Anawrahta's time, when enthusiasm for Theravada Buddhism was so great, these two heresies would seem terrible and grievous. However, they were not the beliefs of a depraved and special school of Buddhism, for they conformed to the two main unorthodox doctrines in support of which the Mahayana school originally broke away from the Theravada school, namely, that in the interpretation of the scriptures the spirit was more important than the actual letter,[1] and that one could reach *Nibbana* by faith in the Buddha alone and the mere invocation of his name. The very name Ari is merely a derivative of the Pali

---

[1] In other words, in interpreting the scriptures they would look beyond the actual text. Therefore, they held that the commentaries were as important as the scriptures. The criticism that 'they wrote books after their own heart' refers surely to the Mahayana commentaries.

term *Ariya* meaning the 'Noble Ones'; and as this term *Ariya* is applicable only to the Buddhist clergy, it follows that Aris were Buddhist monks.

The Aris were described by the Chronicles as heavy drinkers of toddy-wine. It is true, of course, that when toddy- or rice-wine is being offered to the *Nats* there is a ritual drinking of wine among the devotees, and as the Aris were also *Nat* worshippers it is possible that they also took part in the ritual wine-drinking. But there is also the possibility that the Chronicles were echoing an older prejudice against Mahayana monks. One of the points of controversy in Asoka's time between the orthodox and unorthodox schools was over the drinking of unfermented or sweet toddy-wine, the unorthodox school holding that it was not an intoxicant and could, therefore, be consumed by monks.[1]

Various theories concerning the Aris

I may mention some of the existing theories regarding the Aris which, in my opinion, are no longer tenable. According to one theory the name 'Ari' is derived from the Pali term *Arannika* or *Arannavasi*, meaning 'dwellers in the forest', but this theory is not acceptable as the Aris dwelt in great monasteries and not in the forest. Of course there have always been Buddhist monks who shunned the corporate life of a monastery and preferred to dwell in the forest; Kassapa himself, during the Buddha's lifetime, chose to live in this way. In thirteenth-century Pagan many Burmese monks forsook the teeming monasteries of the towns for small 'forest-monasteries' made of bamboo and thatch, which gave them bare shelter from the wind and rain; but in no way were they associated with the Aris of some two centuries earlier.

According to another theory the Aris were Brahmanical

---

[1] This was one of the Ten Indulgences claimed by the 'Monks of Vesali' at the Second Buddhist Council, held about one hundred years after the Buddha's passing away, but the actual emergence of Mahayana schools took place only after the Third Council of Asoka's time.

hermits or ascetics who were worshippers of Vishnu, but who also worshipped the Buddha as a reincarnation of Vishnu. The Burmese word for hermit is *Ya-thay*, which is a derivative of the Sanskrit word *Rishi*; but the Burmese *Ya-thay* is merely an ascetic who has renounced the world for the forest; he is dressed in robes stained dark-brown by home-made dyes from tree-bark and he wears a conical hat over his closely-cut hair. It is true that the Ari monks also wore the same sort of robes and that their heads also were not clean-shaven. But the Burmese have always clearly distinguished the hermit from the monk and in the Chronicles, also, this distinction is clearly drawn.

Burma was the one country in south-east Asia where Hinduism failed to penetrate deeply. Though images of Brahmanical gods have been found both at Prome and Pagan, their number is very small when compared to the thousands of images of the Buddha and Buddhist votive-offerings that have also been found. Moreover, Brahmin astrologers were in the service of the king both at Prome and Pagan and, in addition, there were settlements of Hindu merchants. Doubtless, both astrologers and merchants must have brought their images of Hindu gods. Thus the Hindu images that have been found do not prove that Hinduism was prevalent at Pagan, just as some images of Mahayanist gods and goddesses that have been found at both Prome and Pagan do not by themselves support the theory now advanced in these pages that the Aris were Mahayanist monks. As we have seen, not all the gods of Hinduism were known to the Burmese, and even the cult of Vishnu, the most popular of the Hindu gods, was a mere adjunct of the cult of astrology. Even before Anawrahta the Burmese Vishnu had developed a personality very different from the Indian original.

A theory has also been advanced by some scholars that the Aris were Tantric Buddhists. Of course, Tantric Buddism itself developed out of Mahayana Buddhism, and as the Ari monks were known to have practised magic and sorcery, at first sight it might seem logical to classify them as Tantric Buddhists. However, the magic and sorcery that they patronized were native in origin, and the *Mantra*, which is so important in Tantric magic, has always held a very subordinate position in Burmese magic. It is true that some Tantric frescoes have been found near Pagan, but those frescoes were later than the eleventh century and, therefore, could not have been connected with the Aris, unless they were meant as political propaganda justifying Anawrahta's persecution of the Ari monks some years before.

The worship of the Future Buddha

The worship of the Future Buddha, Metteyya, who is now living in the abode of the gods, has been prevalent in Burma for centuries. The details of his life when he becomes the Buddha, as given in the Commentaries, are so well known to the Burmese that he is known to them as Arit-Metteyya.[1] His images have been found at Pagan. Many Burmese, especially the kings, prayed to be like the Buddha, and at the present day also many devout Burmese still pray to become a Buddha at some distant future. However, the worship of the Future Buddha does not seem to have become a cult in Burma. The worship of a Future Buddha, by itself, is not a Mahayanist 'heresy'. Even in Ceylon, where Theravada Buddhism has had a more or less continuous history, kings set up for worship statues of the Future Buddha 'fifteen cubits high'[2]; and in all Theravada countries, devout Buddhists piously hope to be able to worship the Buddha Metteyya in person and listen to his preaching when he appears.

However, there still exist traces of other Mahayana cults. As has been seen in Chapter 2, the chief disciples of the Buddha who possessed unusual magical and supernatural

---

[1] For the future Buddha will have the personal name of Ajita.
[2] E.g., King Dappula I in the seventh century A.D.

powers were chosen for worship along with the Nine Gods, and that might have been an echo of some Mahayanist cults. In addition, there still exist two cults which are distinctly Mahayanist in origin, namely, the worship of the *Arahat* Shin Thiwali (in Pali *Sivali*), and the worship of the *Arahat* Shin Upagote (in Pali *Upagupta*).

Shin Thiwali

Shin Thiwali was the son of a king's daughter, and he had to remain in his mother's womb for seven long years because of a sin [1] in a past existence. Then for one whole week the mother could not give birth, and on the seventh day she said to her father, the king, 'Let me offer some gifts to the Buddha before I die.' The gifts were made and the Buddha blessed her. Her suffering ceased and she gave birth to Thiwali, who at once spoke and behaved like an adult. The Buddha's Chief Disciple, Shin Sariputtra, arrived on the scene and, receiving permission from the parents admitted Thiwali to the Order. He attained *Arahat*ship the same day. Because of his meritorious deeds in the past he was always receiving gifts of food and robes, and was declared by the Buddha to be the foremost recipient of gifts among his disciples. The Burmese believe that he is still living, that he can be invoked to come by a prayer of special formula and that his mere invisible presence will bring them prosperity and good fortune. Therefore, a tiny image of him, carrying a staff in one hand and a fan in the other, as if ready for travel, is kept for worship in many Burmese households.

Shin Upagote

Shin Upagote seems to have been an entire creation of Mahayana Buddhism, unless he was the same monk as Moggaliputta-Tissa, who presided over the Third Buddhist

[1] Sin, in the Buddhist sense, of a deed which will have evil consequences in one's future existences.

Council, as some scholars would maintain. Shin Upagote was believed to have tamed the arch enemy of Buddhism, the great God Mara himself. Asoka was preparing to hold a great festival in honour of the religion, and the monks, realizing that God Mara would do everything in his power to destroy the festival, sent for Upagote. Upagote, by his miraculous powers, not only defeated Mara in a great struggle, but also converted him to Buddhism. The Burmese believe that Shin Upagote still lives in a floating brazen palace in the southern ocean, and that he too can be invoked to come by a prayer of special formula, and that his mere invisible presence will prevent storms and floods. Some believe also that he can be invoked when danger in the form of some physical violence threatens.

Anuruddha

There was probably also a cult round the personality of *Arahat* Anuruddha, another important disciple of the Buddha. He, too, was famous for his magical and supernatural powers, and Anawrahta himself was named after him. 'Anawrahta' is the Burmese pronunciation of the Pali name 'Anuruddha'. The Burmese Chronicles always spell his Pali name as Anuruddha, but his inscriptions always spell it as Aniruddha, which has puzzled many scholars. In fact, there is no mystery here, for the Mahayana texts always refer to *Arahat* Anuruddha as Aniruddha.

The New Era

According to the Chronicles the Pyus at Prome used the Buddhist Era until A.D. 80, when they introduced a new era, later known as the Pyu Era. They counted this date as the year 2, because officially the New Era began with retrospective effect in A.D. 78. The New Era was established, the Chronicles explained, because A.D. 78 marked the end of an astrological period, and the time when the lunar and solar years nearly coincided. Five hundred and sixty years later, in A.D. 640, the Burmese at Pagan, who had been using the Pyu Era, abandoned it and started a new Burmese Era of their own at the year 2. Again the reason given was that in A.D. 638 another astrological period had ended, and again the lunar and solar years nearly coincided.

However, in A.D. 80 there was another reason besides the astrological one for a change of eras, because in A.D. 78 there was held a Great Buddhist Council under the patronage of the Kushan King, Kaniska. This Great Council, which met in North India, was later denied recognition by the Theravada School, but at the time when the Council was actually being held it was hoped by all Buddhists that the Council would end all existing controversies and various Buddhist sects would unite again. In actual fact, however, Mahayana sects emerged victorious at the Council, which came to be recognized only by the Mahayana School as the Fourth Great Council. An expansion of Mahayana Buddhism in south-east Asia immediately followed, and a new era, dating from this Fourth Great Council, came to be adopted not only in India, but also in south-east Asia. So it may well be that Mahayana Buddhism penetrated the kingdom of Prome, although for a short period only. The excavations at Prome have proved beyond doubt that Theravada Buddhism was the religion that prevailed in the Pyu kingdom. But during the short period of its sudden bloom at Prome the Mahayana sect must have been able to propagate its doctrines to Upper Burma. Of course, Mahayanist ideas could also have come from India overland.

The decay of Buddhism

As mentioned above, the Chronicles maintain that Buddhism in Upper Burma started to decay in the sixth century; the so-called 'decay' must have been the victory of the Mahayana School, for even in A.D. 800 Buddhism in Upper

Burma was far from debased. Chinese historical texts, written about A.D. 800, describe a kingdom in Upper Burma where the standard of morality among the people was high, where astrology was studied and practised, and where Buddhist monasteries numbered over a hundred.[1] It was a Pyu kingdom, the Chinese texts say, but we must remember that even in the thirteenth century, long after the Pyus had disappeared, the Chinese continued to call the Burmese 'Pyu'. However, even if it was not a Burmese kingdom and was, in fact, a Pyu kingdom, it will be difficult to believe that this tradition of morality and religious fervour was not passed on to the neighbouring Burmese kingdom of Pagan.

In the same Chinese texts the following observations are made: 'When they come to the age of seven, both boys and girls drop their hair and stop in a monastery, where they take refuge in the *Sangha*. On reaching the age of twenty, if they have not awoken to the principles of the Buddha, they let their hair grow again and become ordinary townsfolk.' The passage does not say whether the nuns and girl-novices had their own monasteries, but surely the texts would not have described the morality of the people as 'high' if there were no separate monasteries. Conversely, if there were no separate monasteries for nuns and their novices, it will be difficult to accept the statement that the girl-novices were allowed to remain in the monastery beyond the age of puberty. Although some of the details may not be correct, the observation as a whole must be accepted as substantially correct. If we then accept the statement as true, it is clear that the practice of sending young boys and girls to the monastery for a general education, followed by an initiation ceremony when they attained the age of puberty, was already in existence before the days of the kingdom of Pagan.

The people of Pagan doubtless continued this practice, and the phrases 'sending-the-first-flower-to-the-monastery' or

[1] G. H. Luce, 'The Ancient Pyu', *J.B.R.S.*, vol. 27, 1937, p. 251.

'sending-to-the-monastery' merely meant the sending of young children to the monastery, and not the sending of virgins for initiation. This practice was also continued when the Aris had been replaced by the monks of Theravada Buddhism, but perhaps because of the propaganda and resulting prejudice, or perhaps because the monks of Theravada Buddhism were more strict in the matter of accepting even young girls in the monastery, girls were no longer sent to the monastery for their education. This is my view regarding the 'flower-sending ceremonies' of the Chronicles, for I think that the Chronicles stoop to political propaganda in describing the beliefs and practices of the Aris. However, I admit the possibility that the *droit de seigneur* of the Ari monks really existed and, if it did, it must have arisen out of the primitive elements present in the initiation ceremonies.

It may well be that after its victory in Upper Burma in the sixth century, Mahayanist Buddhism bloomed for some centuries and then swiftly decayed as the primitive cults which it had first controlled and patronized finally corrupted and overwhelmed it, so that by the eleventh century its Ari monks were Buddhists only in name, and Anawrahta and the new Theravada Buddhism had no place for them. The easy catholic doctrines of the old Mahayana School, the ascetic and strict doctrines of the new Theravada School, the lax and tolerant attitude of the Ari monks, and the uncompromising and impatient discipline of Anawrahta are well contrasted in the following folk-tale account of Anawrahta's visit to the Chinese kingdom of Gandalarit (Yunnan),[1] although no specific mention is made of Mahayana or Ari monks.

'So the Great King Anawrahta, attended by his four commanders and the Brothers Inferior Gold, arrived at the Golden City of Gandalarit. Anawrahta went to the monastery of the Royal Chaplain and the King was undecided whether to

[1] A more sober account is given in the Chronicles. See Tin & Luce, op. cit., p. 81.

worship him or not. "Is he a hermit or a monk?" mused the Great King. "He wears dark brown robes and he has a rosary in his hand, but he is surrounded by thousands of retainers, and he is strong and fat." The King's Chaplain on his own part was puzzled because dressed alike in fine raiment and mounted on demon horses, the King and his six mighty men looked exactly alike, and he did not know who was the leader of the seven. So he placed seven golden chairs for his visitors to sit on. Anawrahta became angry and, shouting "I am the King," hit the seven chairs with the flat of his lance and at once the seven chairs became one and he sat down in it. "Ascetic," exclaimed the King, "I am the Great Anawrahta of Pagan, and go and tell your King that I have come to take away the Tooth Relic of our Lord, the Buddha." The Royal Chaplain went and informed the King of Gandalarit, but the latter remained in his palace, keeping Anawrahta waiting for seven whole days. Losing patience, Anawrahta went again to the Royal Chaplain and asked, "You and your King, are you Buddhists, or are you heathens? For your well-being in this existence and in future existences, whom do you worship?" "Great King," replied the Royal Chaplain, "for our well-being in future existences, we worship the Buddha and his Tooth Relic, but for our well-being in the present life, we worship the Great God, Sanni, and his copper image, one hundred *viss* in weight." "Where is the Tooth Relic and where is the image?" asked the surprised Anawrahta. "The Tooth Relic is well hidden in a secret chamber," explained the Royal Chaplain, "but the image of God Sanni is kept in a golden shrine in front of the palace, for all to worship." Anawrahta quickly went to the golden shrine, and ordered Kyansittha and the Brothers Inferior Gold to tie a rope round the neck of the image and pull it down. After the copper image had been pulled down, Anawrahta mercilessly beat it with the flat of his lance and the image shouted out in fear and in pain, "Oh, King of Gandalarit, for your well-being

in this life and for my well-being also, worship the Great
Patron of Buddhism, the mighty King Anawrahta.'''

The smouldering ashes

Although Anawrahta's attitude towards the older faiths
was harsh and intolerant, it will be wrong to assume that he
forced the new Theravada Buddhism down the throats of his
people. On the contrary, the majority of his people had no
doubt that the new religion was far nobler and purer. But,
like a housewife who had bought a new lamp yet found it
difficult to throw away the old one, Anawrahta's people,
basking in the light of the new faith, still had some attach-
ment for the old. Again, in spite of Anawrahta's uncompromising discipline and his cruel persecution of the old faiths,
their ashes continued to smoulder and burn faintly in the
remoter regions of the country.

As stated above, King Kyansittha eased the burden of
religious persecution. Although under his strong rule and the
rule of his immediate successor the ashes of the old faiths
could only smoulder, when weaker kings followed, from the
same ashes there arose faint flames, and occasionally there
were even strong indications that organized sects of monks,
lax in their morals but strong in popularity because of their
avowed mastery of magic, alchemy and spirit worship, could
dare challenge the authority of the established school of
Buddhism. But with the passing of time the ashes ceased to
smoulder, and long before Kubla Khan's army came knocking
at the gates the Theravada Buddhism in Burma found itself
without any rival.

During the period of stress and uncertainty that intervened between the fall of Pagan and the establishment of a
strong dynasty at Ava, the good name of the Buddhist clergy
was stained by the insatiable thirst for toddy-wine on the
part of many leading monks who surrounded the soldiers of
fortune who had carved out the great Pagan empire into

small kingdoms for themselves. However, it will not be correct to say that those monks were Aris and that the old Mahayana Buddhism had reappeared like a phoenix. Admittedly, they might have revived memories of the old Aris in the minds of the people, but in reality they were merely the weeds that naturally appeared in the neglected garden of the national religion, and they were easily plucked when the new gardener, in the person of a strong king, came to the golden throne of Ava.

BIBLIOGRAPHY

Aung, Maung Htin. 'Alchemy and Alchemists in Burma'. *Folk Lore*, 1933.

Aung, Maung Htin. *Burmese Drama*. Oxford University Press, 1937.

Aung, Maung Htin. *Burmese Folk-Tales*. Oxford University Press, 1948.

Burlingame, E. W. *Buddhist Legends*, Part II. Harvard Oriental Series, 1921.

Conze, Edward. *The Buddha*. Bruno Cassirer, Oxford, 1953.

Grant Brown, W. F. 'The Taungbyon Festival'. *Journal of the Royal Anthropological Institute*, 1915.

Grant Brown, W. F. 'The Dragon of Tagaung'. *Journal of the Royal Asiatic Society*, 1917.

Grant Brown, W. F. 'The Pre-Buddhist Religion of the Burmese'. *Folk-Lore*, 1921.

Harvey, G. E. *History of Burma*. Longmans, London, 1925.

Hmannan Yazawin. *The Glass Palace Chronicle of the Kings of Burma* (in Burmese), (Vols. 1 to V). Upper Burma Press, Mandalay, 1908. (Vol. I has been translated into English by Pe Maung Tin & G. H. Luce. Oxford, 1923.)

Kyar, U Po. *The Thirty-Seven Nats* (in Burmese). Myanma Gonyee Press, Rangoon, 1937.

Luce, G. H. 'The Ancient Pyu'. *Journal of the Burma Research Society*, 1937.

Rockhill, W. Woodwille. *The Life of Buddha*. Kegan Paul, London, 1907.

Shin Arseinnabiwuntha. *Buddhist Prayers*. Light of Knowledge Press, Rangoon, 1954.

Temple, Sir R. C. *The Thirty-Seven Nats*. Griggs, London, 1906.

Thomas, Edward, J. *The Life of Buddha*. Kegan Paul, London, 1956.

Zinattapakathanikyan. *Life of Buddha* (in Burmese). Hanthawaddy Press, Rangoon, 1910.

Printed in Great Britain
Spottiswoode, Ballantyne & Co. Ltd.
London and Colchester